GETTING
REAL

Other books by Susan M. Campbell, Ph.D.

Beyond the Power Struggle
The Couple's Journey
Earth Community
Expanding Your Teaching Potential
From Chaos to Confidence

GETTING
REAL

SUSAN CAMPBELL, Ph.D.

FOREWORD BY BRAD BLANTON, Ph.D.

An H J Kramer Book

published in a joint venture with

New World Library

An H J Kramer Book
published in a joint venture with
New World Library

Editorial office:	Administrative office:
H J Kramer	New World Library
P.O. Box 1082	14 Pamaron Way
Tiburon, California 94920	Novato, California 94949

Cover design by Mary Beth Salmon
Text design by Mary Ann Casler

Library of Congress Cataloging-in-Publication Data
Campbell, Susan M., 1941–
  Getting real : the ten truth skills you need to live an authentic life /
  by Susan M. Campbell.
     p.   cm.
  Includes bibliographical references and index.
  ISBN 0-915811-92-8 (perfect : alk. paper)
  1. Self-actualization (Psychology) I. Title.
BF637.S4 C343 2001
158—dc21   00-013263

First Printing, April 2001
ISBN 0-915811-92-8
Printed in Canada on acid-free paper
Distributed to the trade by Publishers Group West

10 9 8 7 6 5 4 3 2

On personal integrity hangs humanity's fate.
— Buckminster Fuller

CONTENTS

ACKNOWLEDGMENTS

I would like to express my love and gratitude to my mother and father, who first encouraged me to listen to and trust my inner voice. I can still hear my mother's words, delivered in her slow southern drawl as I toddled off to my first day of kindergarten, "Remember, Susan, that teacher's not the boss o' you." She continues to support my uniqueness to this day.

I am deeply grateful to my friend Robert Chaffey, who by his example has given me the courage to become more transparent in both my private and public life. He has been my greatest teacher.

I am blessed to have many creative friends who have read and critiqued various versions of the manuscript. Many thanks to Tom Huntington, Pam Astarte, Dan Fox, Robert Willard, Brad Blanton, Liz Craig, Dean LaCoe, Susan Bradley, Greg Small, Peller Marion, and Flo Hoylman. I am grateful to Kenn Burrows for introducing me to the term *relating* and to Padi Selwyn for offering me the title *Getting Real*.

I owe so much to my early teachers: Fritz Perls, Marilyn Rosanes-Beret, Erv Polster, Miriam Polster, Robert Resnick, Jim Simkin, Bernie Gunther, Charlotte Selver, Steve Tobin, and Virginia Satir, and to my more recent teachers: Brad Blanton, Paul Lowe, and Dhiravamsa. The challenging support I have received from these gifted mentors has enabled me to offer a similar type of mentoring to others.

Much appreciation also goes to the wonderful people at H J Kramer/New World Library, who have helped me prepare the book for publication: Linda Kramer, Hal Kramer, Georgia Hughes, and Mimi Kusch.

FOREWORD

Those of us who understand honesty as a fundamental spiritual practice know that simply being honest, like meditation, helps us to experience life more fully. Whether we're meditating alone or being honest when sharing with others, we find that a natural ease, happiness, and love occurs when we simply pay attention and notice what is going on rather than thinking about it. In fact, a further magnification of the already enhanced experience of being that comes from noticing occurs when we accurately describe our experience of noticing to another. Intimacy happens. Two beings know each other and have learned more about *being* itself. Rather than getting smarter, this process involves getting simpler, even "dumber." Come to think of it, paying attention to paying attention is really kind of a dumb idea itself. Luckily for us, Susan Campbell has written a pretty dumb book to explain this dumb idea to us. In this dumb book she says some really wise things: We don't have to protect ourselves all the time, like we all learned to do in order to survive, because "we're big now." Although it seems as if most of us should get that, most of us don't most of the time. It's too simple for a mind to get.

Susan also says, "In most human interactions, relating is preferable to controlling because it brings you into the present." Ain't it the truth — and too few of us get to discover that truth before we die. Susan believes we human beings are "evolving beyond control-oriented communication." God, I hope so. This fine book provides guidelines for "getting real" as an alternative to merely "being right." (Susan has the best of both worlds because she gets to "be right" about "getting real.")

I love Susan Campbell. She has been a part of our Radical Honesty cult for about five years now. A lot of what she says in this book she learned by being honest as a personal practice and from being with other honest people. We are some of the dumbest people you would ever want to meet. Now, mind you, we're not completely cured of our smartness. We still have to remind each other about how smartness blocks wisdom. We still need to practice all the time to stay grounded in noticing so some wisdom occurs, now and then, more or less of its own accord. With this book, Susan has used her smartness in service to what she has learned through noticing like a dummie. It is a way to heal herself. It's a recovery program. She has done a beautiful job. Lucky for us, we get to come along.

— Brad Blanton, Ph.D.,
author of *Radical Honesty*

INTRODUCTION

As you, the reader, and I, the author, embark on this exploration of how to live authentically, I'd like to share some experiences that have led me to be so passionate about this topic. I grew up in a happy home with wonderful parents and three siblings who loved and supported me, and still I'm as screwed up as everybody else! My ability to be authentically myself started getting compromised just after I was born. That was when I started taking on a bunch of false beliefs about how the world works and how people are. From piecing together the details of my early life, based on my parents' accounts, here's how I figure that happened.

The Story of My Personality

When my mom tried to nurse me, her milk did not come down. As a hungry infant, I sucked and sucked, harder and harder, trying to get the nourishment I needed. No matter how hard I sucked, nothing came. I felt frustrated and empty, and there seemed to be nothing I could do to escape that feeling of emptiness. I was afraid, bewildered, alone, and in pain. And my mom felt pain, too, but hers was the pain of having her nipples ravaged. So she took me from her breast and put a bottle in my mouth. This critical incident created in my little mind what I now call false belief #1: if you express your wants too strongly, you'll get punished.

My mom still held me in her arms often, but when our bodies were close, she could feel in me a restless energy that never seemed to be satisfied. She tried to comfort me and to help me feel safe, but her efforts were futile. Since I was her firstborn, she was quite vulnerable to self-doubts about her adequacy as a mother. Sensing this, I feared making her feel even more uncomfortable. So I tried to deal with my restless dissatisfaction within myself. The solution I discovered was to sleep most of the time, which kept everybody "happy." Thus evolved false belief #2: you need to shut down your feelings to avoid making others uncomfortable.

Then my father entered the picture. He and I bonded right away. He loved to hold and play with me. My favorite game was when he would "capture" me, surrounding me gently with his big body so I couldn't get away. This game was scary in a really delightful way.

About that time World War II was being fought, and my dad was called into service. I didn't know what was going on as my parents prepared for his departure, but I could sense in my mom a deep sadness as she anticipated her loss. On a gray day in November 1944, the three of us drove to the train station to see my dad off. I was pretty silent until the very last moments before he got on the train. At that point I put all the pieces together and realized what was happening. As he slowly walked away from us, I started screaming, "Daddy, don't go! Daddy, don't go!" But in spite of my protests, he was on his way, and false belief #3 was hatched: no matter how much you want something, even if you holler about it, you won't get it. This is especially true when you really, really want it.

My mom and I survived just fine, eventually Dad came home, and our life became routine again. At this point, I was starting grammar school. For me it was a time of being very observant of and curious

about everything and everyone and being fascinated with the similari-
ties and differences among people. I noticed something about my dad
that disturbed me greatly. He had what we called in my family "his
temper." He was embarrassed and apologetic about this characteristic,
but that didn't keep me from feeling fearful every time he raised his
voice at me: "Susan, stop your youncing!" I can still hear him snapping
at me when my demands for attention would start to bother him.
(Even though beliefs #1 and #2 prohibited bothering others, those
beliefs only applied to the really deep and important needs. I could still
be incessant about petty things.)

My dad's temper flare-ups scared me — even though I now
know that they were relatively mild compared to those of some
other dads. But I was becoming a smart little kid, so instead of feeling my fear, I quickly learned that it was more comfortable to have
inner conversations about how stupid his outbursts were. I recall
thinking to myself, "He got so worked up over such a small thing."
Once or twice I even voiced my criticisms: my dad was going on
loudly about "what could have happened" as a result of something
I'd done, and I had the audacity to shout back, "Well it could've
happened, but it didn't!" Probably the second or third time I did
that, I got a slap across the mouth. Out of these experiences came
false beliefs #4 and #5: you can avoid painful feelings by becoming
judgmental or critical of others; and it's not safe to talk back to an
angry person. It's better just to keep cool.

Along the path of my life, I have picked up a few more dysfunctional beliefs, but these five will do to give you an idea of how I
learned that it's not safe to feel and express your true feelings. My story
also shows how I learned strategies for staying safe and in control: by
not expressing wants or anger and by being judgmental when I was
really afraid. I spent the years that followed perfecting these strategies.
The result was that even though there was a deeply feeling, caring, loving, hurting, fearful human being in there somewhere, what I mostly

showed to the world during much of my life was the competent, intelligent, helpful, overcontrolled good girl. This is why I'm so passionate about the practice of Getting Real — because for so much of my life I occupied only a few of the many rooms of my emotional house.

As a psychotherapist for the past thirty-four years, I have, of course, observed that I am not alone in this game of limiting ourselves in the interests of staying safe. It is part of the human journey to start out whole, then to continually cut off parts of ourselves in response to real or imagined pain, and to spend the rest of our lives searching for what we have cut off, buried, and forgotten about. Even entire cultures seem to operate within a very narrow band of the total human experience. Thus, we project onto others what we cannot feel, experience, and own up to in ourselves. War and conflict are the result, when all the while we long for peace.

Getting Real is about reclaiming, reviving, and reexperiencing these buried parts of ourselves. In my own journey I have studied and applied many methods toward this end. After years of exploration, I have found that the quickest and best route to wholeness is honest communication with yourself and others. Of course, in attempting to follow this simple prescription, you will come up against all the ways you have cut yourself off from the truth of your existence. So honest communication becomes your "awareness practice" — your vehicle for noticing what you avoid (your irrational fears) and how you go about avoiding it (your control patterns).

> Honest communication becomes your "awareness practice" — your vehicle for noticing what you avoid (your irrational fears) and how you go about avoiding it (your control patterns).

Using Honesty to Stay with Your Experience

Honest communication is not only the quickest, most direct path to wholeness, it is also the least expensive. Without spending years in a therapist's office, you can learn a set of communication practices that will lead you to the truth of your present experience and out of the morass of judgments, generalizations, shoulds, withholdings, assessments, and explanations about why you are the way you are. These practices are a way of using language to help you stay with your present felt experience — what you see, hear, smell, feel, remember, sense, and intuit. You can learn these practices in a relatively short time period, since so many other explorers have already charted the way. Buddhist meditation practice, Gestalt therapy, Jungian analysis, sensory awareness, Reichian and bioenergetic body work — these are the main underpinnings of the work that I call Getting Real.

> These practices are a way of using language to help you stay with your present felt experience.

The reason honest communication works so well as a growth path is that most of the time, when you go deeply and patiently into an experience, feeling it fully without escaping into a control pattern, it changes! I'm not kidding. The way out is to go deeply in. You will discover this truth for yourself as you engage in the practices — I call them the ten truth skills — suggested in this book. Some of these skills take quite a bit of courage. Others actually ease the way and make honesty less threatening. When you use them in combination, you will find that they support one another and make the whole process of being honest quite enlivening and less frightening than you might imagine.

The Getting Real process will go faster if you have a skilled coach or teacher to help you avoid the pitfalls of self-deception, and it absolutely requires at least one or two committed others who agree to undertake this journey with you. So after you read this book, be sure to share it with anyone who might be a likely candidate for the role of "committed other."

Getting Real has worked and still works for me and for the

hundreds of others I have coached in this method. As I continue to do this work, I keep learning that we human beings have far more potential than we give ourselves credit for: there is so much more love that we could feel, so much more reality that we could perceive, so much more excitement and energy that we could contain and vibrate with. All we need is genuine curiosity, an openness to experiment, and a willingness to experience with awareness whatever comes up. The prize you will attain for this effort is a deep and abiding trust in yourself and in life that no one can ever take away from you.

> All we need is genuine curiosity, an openness to experiment, and a willingness to experience with awareness whatever comes up.

Getting Real develops your self-awareness. You engage with others in what I call a social meditation practice in which you support one another in unhooking from your self-image and your ideas about being "better" and risk being seen just as you are. The result is self-realization — making real the parts of yourself that you thought you had to hide to survive. And I mean *all* the parts, not just the pretty ones. Self-realization also leads you back to the simple, direct awareness of yourself as a being increasingly free of your personal story and the limiting beliefs you've picked up along the way. But before you can be free of these, you need to be willing to explore, experiment, and discover where your natural flow of energy is blocked. And to free yourself, you need to experience just how unfree you are.

We're All Hypocrites

As far back as I can remember, I've been on a campaign to expose the fact that we're all hypocrites to one degree or another. We live in a world that challenges our sense of integrity at every turn. We say we value a clean environment, but we drive cars and ride in airplanes. We say we value democracy, but we secretly want our own way. We say we value honesty, but we frequently withhold our true feelings to avoid conflict. We all preach one thing and practice another. Learning to live in the gap between our ideals and our reality seems to be the koan of our age. This process is the true meaning of sobriety — the ability to honestly face the reality of our predicament without projecting blame onto some outside force and without looking for some magical rescue from the challenges of living with integrity.

In my years of experience as a psychotherapist, teamwork consultant, speaker, and seminar leader, I've found that it's much more rewarding in the long run to notice and soberly accept *what is* than to focus so much of our attention on what should be. Shoulds prevent us from seeing how our life really is — and from taking appropriate action. Shoulds are pretenses. Telling yourself that you "should be more generous" is a way of hoodwinking yourself and others into thinking that you want to be generous. Shoulds also justify not taking action in a situation that has become intolerable. "He shouldn't treat me that way." So you focus on what he should or shouldn't do instead of on your own anger, and you get to feel wronged, righteous, and stuck. Shoulds keep you from owning your power to create the life you want. They keep you in denial about your actual feelings and situation.

> Shoulds prevent us from seeing how our life really is — and from taking appropriate action. Shoulds are pretenses.

Getting Real serves as an antidote to the sort of self-deception that keeps people feeling powerless and overwhelmed. Once you stop trying to get reality to conform to your ideas and ideals and let yourself see, feel, and express *what is*, you will feel more empowered to deal effectively with your present situation. You won't be stuck anymore or clogged up with unfinished business. You'll be participating

in this vast evolutionary dance called life. You'll learn to trust yourself to handle whatever comes your way — because you won't be limited by your ideas about what
should happen. You'll be open
to discovering what each new
situation brings out of you.
You'll be living your uniqueness. Your path will have heart.

In this process you may fall
down and get hurt at times,
like when you were learning to ride a bicycle. But when you get up
and dust yourself off, you'll see that along with the pain, there is
a beautiful new experience that you might never have had if you
hadn't been open to it.

> Once you stop trying to get reality
> to conform to your ideas and ideals
> and let yourself see, feel, and
> express what is, you will feel more
> empowered to deal effectively
> with your present situation.

You're Okay Just As You Are

From leading Getting Real workshops, I have learned how free
people feel when they notice, feel, and express their own inner experience, agreeing for a day or two to set aside their normal conven-
tions of politeness and appropriateness. Most people are amazed to
discover that they feel okay just as they are — warts and all. My purpose in writing this book is to help you see that wherever you are on
your life path, you may as well relax and stop trying to be somewhere else. This is *what is*. I enjoin you to stop fighting *what is* so
that you can:

1. relax and enjoy yourself
2. deal realistically and creatively with the truth of your existence
   (instead of waiting to take action until you're "better" or until
   someone else does what they're supposed to do)
3. allow yourself to be seen and loved (realizing that you are
   most lovable when you are most transparent)

4. be present to each moment of your life (uninhibited by your judging and comparing mind telling you that you're not enough)

5. trust yourself to "cross future bridges when you come to them" (rather than worrying about something you cannot predict or control)

6. feel peaceful and self-accepting (most of the time)

The work of Getting Real is about paying attention to and communicating about what you notice — your bodily sensations, your feelings, your thoughts, and the things going on around you. When I use the term *work,* I do not mean to imply struggle. I do not mean exerting. I do not mean working against yourself.

> You are most lovable when you are most transparent.

If you notice yourself doing these things, pay attention. Your power to heal any tendency to struggle against yourself lies in your ability to be aware of *what is,* without praise or blame. The simple act of being aware gives you tremendous freedom. Your freedom will be even greater if you share with others how you experience your awareness. I like to say that freedom's just another word for nothing left to hide. I invite you to come out of hiding and to reconnect with your essential freedom, aliveness, and trust in yourself and others.

To help create a playful, nonthreatening environment in which to practice Getting Real, I have invented two card games: I think it's important to enjoy ourselves while we're learning and working. The first one, the Getting Real Card Game, can be played with several friends or family members. It's a great way to have fun while practicing the ten truth skills. The other, called the Truth at Work Card Game, is for people in the workplace. I have been using this game successfully in conjunction with my team-building and communication-training business for several years. You can order these games from me by using the order form in appendix C.

I also do phone and on-line coaching and lead one- and two-day Getting Real workshops for work teams and the general public, as well as a two-day workshop for couples. If the playful work of Getting Real speaks to you, please contact me for more information. I would be happy to come to your location to offer a workshop or training program. Susan Campbell, 4373 Hessel Ct., Sebastopol, CA 95472. Phone: (707) 829-3646. E-mail: drsusan@susancampbell.com. Websites: www.susancampbell.com and ww.thegettingrealgame.com.

How This Book Is Organized

The main body of the book, chapters 2 through 11, are devoted to describing the ten truth skills and showing you how and when to use them. Each of these chapters includes a self-assessment quiz to help you see how comfortable you are in the domain of the truth skill being considered. The chapters also contain stories of real people (whose names and identifying details have been altered) who have learned to use the skills successfully, as well as exercises that you can do alone or with a partner to give you practice using each skill. Each chapter concludes with a short summation of key points under the heading "In a Nutshell."

The appendices at the end of the book contain further resources to support the process of Getting Real. In appendix A, you will find a list of related books and seminars. Appendix B contains the communication guidelines that I use in my seminars with instructions on how you can start your own group using these guidelines. Appendix C includes descriptions of the two interactive card games I have created that you can purchase and play with your friends or coworkers. It also contains ordering information and a page that you can use for ordering.

HOW TO STOP BEING RIGHT AND START BEING REAL

1

Have you ever
- been bored listening to someone but acted interested?
- pretended to like someone more than you really did?
- pretended to like someone less than you really did?
- had trouble admitting you didn't know something you're supposed to know?
- had trouble admitting you were wrong?
- had difficulty asking for what you wanted?
- acted happy when you felt sad?
- had difficulty admitting you were attracted to someone until you found out how they felt about you?
- had a problem saying no or marking your boundaries?
- had trouble telling your sexual partner that you're not satisfied?
- reacted defensively when you thought you were being criticized?
- had difficulty expressing your anger, jealousy, or hurt?
- had trouble expressing your love, caring, or vulnerability?
- avoided telling someone something that you feared might be hurtful?

If you answered yes to many of these questions, rest assured that you're not alone: I ask hundreds of people these questions during speeches and seminars, and nearly everyone answers yes to most of them. Yes, we all lie, sugarcoat, pretend, or withhold. Why? The most common reasons people give are

- to avoid hurting people's feelings
- to avoid looking foolish
- to avoid conflict, disagreement, or feeling anger
- to ensure that things turn out right
- to avoid feeling out of control

We lie to avoid whatever we perceive as dangerous — to our ego, to our comfort, to our safety. Most of all we lie because our sense of safety and self-esteem depends on our feeling in control, in control of how other people react to us, of whether we appear smart or foolish, of whether we'll get what we want.

Getting Real at Work

I was giving my first coaching session to an executive from a Fortune 100 company. We were meeting to go over the results of a survey he had given his employees asking for their feedback about his effectiveness as a leader. As soon as we sat down, he disclosed, "I haven't looked at the results of the survey." I had an immediate reaction. I was not pleased! The previous week we had agreed that both of us would study the results of the survey in preparation for this meeting. My body felt flushed and hot. I felt a mixture of anger and disappointment. I was saying to myself, "I wasn't expecting this. I don't want to have this meeting if he's not prepared." Instead I mumbled, "How come? Weren't you interested in what your people had to say about you?"

> Most of all we lie because our sense of safety and self-esteem depends on our feeling in control.

He smiled sheepishly, looked down at the floor, and said something about having too much on his plate. So I feigned sympathy.

Fortunately, at that point in the conversation, I felt the urge to use the restroom, so I excused myself. Standing at the sink in the women's room, I gave myself time to get present to what I was experiencing. I took a few deep breaths and went back to our conference room. I looked my client in the eye and told him, "Leo, I'm feeling angry and disappointed that you didn't read what your people wrote about you." As soon as I said those words, I knew I was going to be okay. I felt a big surge of relief in my body and renewed clarity in my thoughts. I waited for his response. He sat there for several seconds, just looking at me. Then he said something I didn't expect: "Thank you. I needed to hear that." We both heaved a big sigh of relief as I exclaimed, "Well, now that we have that out of the way, shall we get to work?"

My behavior during the first part of the meeting was typical of so many of us. We try to act in control instead of admitting that we're upset or befuddled. Instead of sharing our feelings and thoughts, we try to ensure a predictable outcome (I wanted him to like me, and I wanted the meeting to proceed smoothly). We communicate with the intent to control rather than with the intent to relate. But until we take a risk and share authentically, nothing real can happen.

> When people throw away the script and show up in the moment, suddenly a lot of creative energy is released, and something can get accomplished.

We're like actors reading from a script. When people throw away the script and show up in the moment, suddenly a lot of creative energy is released, and something can get accomplished.

As my meeting with Leo showed me, honest expression of feelings also helps to clear away the fog that clouds our perception of what is — especially when we express something we have been withholding or trying not to think about. Once I expressed my withheld anger, I was able to release those feelings and could then give Leo much more of my attention.

New Human Capacities

In the mid-1990s I conducted a three-year research study of the "new human capacities" that people need to develop to survive and thrive in a world of tumultuous change and information overload. Based on a survey of approximately five hundred people, the research demonstrated that about 80 percent of the average person's communications are geared toward controlling things that are actually beyond the person's control: a huge waste of human energy.

More often than not the truth of a situation doesn't conform to our ideas about how things should be. In the example above, I thought Leo *should* have read the survey results. Where did that get me? Well, it got me behaving in a way that was disconnected from both the truth of the situation and the truth of my own feelings. The truth is often more confusing, paradoxical, uncomfortable, or messy than we might wish it to be. It cannot be controlled. The people in my study who experienced the greatest number of painful unexpected surprises (such as job loss, divorce, and alienation from their grown children) were those who demonstrated the highest need for control. It seems that the more you try to get reality to fit within your comfort zone, the more unprepared you are to deal with a world full of surprise, complexity, and change. Likewise, if we persist in trying to get our relationships to conform to our expectations instead of letting them be how they actually are, we may miss important opportunities to know ourselves and others more deeply.

When I was in high school, my family's dinner conversations often centered on my dad's frustrations with upper management in the company where he worked. Dad was a mid-level manager in a company that manufactured and sold business calculating machines in an era when better-faster-cheaper computers were just about to arrive on the market. My dad was pretty certain that if his company didn't start listening to customers and giving them what they wanted, the company would fold. Every night I would listen to Dad ranting about his bosses — what they should do if they had any brains and what he would do if he were leading the company.

I would often ask him, "Instead of telling *us,* can't you tell *them* what you think? Wouldn't they want to hear what you have to say?"

"Oh no, they'd just say 'don't be so negative.' And then I'd feel even more frustrated."

Reflecting on these conversations, I now view my dad's behavior as a good example of withholding true feelings and thoughts to maintain a sense of control: he had it all figured out. He knew how his bosses should be and how they would react to his ideas. By staying silent, he stayed in control. He never had to risk being disagreed with, criticized, or ignored. He got to stay right where he felt comfortable — wronged, but righteous — to the very end when the company did go under and he could say, "I told you so."

Staying in control, or at least avoiding feeling not in control, is a powerful motivator, to be sure. Recently, however, control-oriented communication (or lack of communication, as in Dad's case) has begun to fall out of favor. More and more people are waking up to the fact that trying to play it safe and to avoid unwanted outcomes has a way of sneaking up on you and biting you in the backside. Those very things you try to avoid get you in the end, so to speak. My dad was trying to avoid the unwanted outcome of being without a job. And where did that behavior get him? He wound up losing his job and his self-respect. He later disclosed, "At least if I had told them what I thought, I'd have my self-respect intact, whether they listened or not. I wish I'd known then what I know now."

In conducting my study, I talked to many people who have

begun to recognize the price they have paid for trying to control things that really are not within their control. Because of the evolutionary forces of information overload and rapid, unpredictable change, we now need to become less attached to how things should turn out and communicate more about what is actually going on — even if doing so is uncomfortable or threatening. Doing so requires that we take our prejudices, preconceptions, and shoulds lightly so that we can accurately perceive the feedback we get rather than having our perceptions clouded by what we expect, what we fear, or what we think should be happening. I call this new orientation toward communication *relating*. Relating is how you get real.

Relating Versus Controlling

Control-oriented communication is geared toward ensuring a predictable result. It is the ego-mind's way of protecting us from feeling anxious or uncomfortable when facing an unexpected or unknown outcome. The ego-mind is that part of us that likes to feel in control. Many of us don't trust that, if we don't get the result we were hoping for, we'll be resourceful enough to come up with a "plan B."

When we relate we value *what is* over what should or could be. When you relate, as opposed to when you control, you speak the truth of what you think, feel, and notice as a way of sharing information and making emotional contact — and not as a way of getting a particular outcome. You speak your truth without knowing how this truth will be received. When I told Leo that I was angry and disappointed, I was taking a risk. He could have told me I was being disrespectful and walked out on me. I was willing to take that chance, because I trusted that whatever happened, I'd be okay. I also knew that if I wasn't truthful with myself and with Leo, all further communication between us would be compromised and that our meeting would not be very productive.

The Ten Truth Skills

This book is a kind of primer for the practice of conscious, deeply contacting communication — the type of communication that pushes you closer to that edge of aliveness where you trust yourself enough to speak your truth even without being sure of how you will be received, where you are relating instead of controlling.

To really experience true contact with another person, you must enter a realm of uncertainty together. To help you gain the courage and confidence to live this way, in this book I describe ten essential life skills, which I call truth skills. In chapters 2 through 11, I discuss each of these ten truth skills in detail. I will outline them here for you briefly.

> To really experience true contact with another person, you must enter a realm of uncertainty together.

1. *Experiencing what is.* When I use the words *what is,* I am referring to whatever is actually going on in the present moment — in your body, in your mind, and in your environment. By noticing and feeling *what is,* you learn to distinguish between what you actually experience in your body and emotions from what your mind thinks, judges, expects, or believes should be happening. This practice will help you communicate about your current reality more accurately and honestly. It will keep you connected to the energy of being alive, thereby training you not to depend so much on external results, such as what others think of you, for your sense of well-being.

2. *Being transparent.* Self-disclosure, or what I am calling being transparent, is the ability to reveal to another person what you have done or what you are sensing, feeling, thinking, or saying to yourself at the moment. When you share your thoughts, sensations, feelings, even your judgments "in the interest of transparency," you are less apt to get caught up in the illusion of control. The motive behind your self-expression is just that — self-expression. It is not about trying to get people to change. As a result, your expression is less likely to

trigger a defensive reaction in them. Letting yourself be seen by others is also an important aid to seeing yourself more honestly. It is harder to fool yourself when you are going public about who you are.

3. *Noticing your intent.* Communicating with the intent to *control* the outcome of a situation represents the ego-mind's efforts to protect you. The intent to control, or to self-protect, does have its place, especially if you are in physical danger. However, most people communicate with the intent to control rather than to *relate* far more than they need to. If you really want to see the reality of a situation or to connect with someone emotionally, you need to allow yourself to be open to the possibilities of each moment — spontaneous and unrehearsed. You need to *relate* more and *control* less.

4. *Welcoming feedback.* Welcoming feedback is another way to be present to *what is.* It means being attuned to what is happening around you each moment. When you welcome feedback, you are actively curious about how others are affected by your actions. You ask, "How are you with what I just did?" or "What is your response to what I'm saying?" Asking for feedback keeps the two-way flow of conversation going, an essential ingredient of relating. The ability to notice others' verbal and nonverbal feedback is how you learn from experience. You do or say something, then you notice what happens. In this way you can see whether your behavior serves your needs, aims, and values.

5. *Asserting what you want and don't want.* Asserting what you want affirms your right to want what you want — even if you imagine it's an unreasonable demand or that there's little chance of getting it. This skill also helps you become less attached to getting everything you ask for, since each request won't carry such a heavy load. When you are free and fluent with your

> Asserting what you want affirms your right to want what you want — even if you imagine it's an unreasonable demand or that there's little chance of getting it.

requests, you don't expect to get everything you ask for. But when you save up your requests for "the really important things," each request carries more significance than is realistic. Asking freely, instead of inhibiting yourself, keeps your energy flowing. You are saying yes to yourself, no matter how another person responds to your wants.

> Asking freely instead of inhibiting yourself, keeps your energy flowing. You are saying yes to yourself, no matter how another person responds to your wants.

It is also very important to let people know about what you don't want. You need to be able to refuse to do, receive, tolerate, or speak about something, if that is your honest response. This kind of asserting may result in the other person being disappointed, frustrated, or angry; but if a relationship is to be authentic, there needs to be space for people to experience their full range of feelings and to have those feelings be okay.

6. *Taking back projections.* Often what you "see" in another person is actually a mirror of something in yourself that you're uncomfortable with. When a timid person is put off by someone aggressive, perhaps she is disowning her own "aggressiveness," that is, her ability to stand up for herself. When a dominating person is bothered by a timid, fearful person, perhaps he is not acknowledging his own fearfulness. The phenomenon of projection has been recognized since ancient times. In the Sermon on the Mount in the Bible, Christ urged his followers to be mindful of noticing the speck in their neighbor's eye while failing to notice the log in their own. Becoming aware of projections helps you to season your judgments with some humility. It can also help you to remember that other people's judgments about you are as much (or more) about them as they are about you. And perhaps most important, this kind of awareness can show you where your life energy is blocked or stuck in a pattern so that you can get it flowing again.

7. *Revising an earlier statement.* We can learn to be flexible enough to change our minds and to let someone know that our feelings have changed. You may at times notice that you no longer feel something after you have expressed it; you may realize hours or days after you have shared something that it was a lie; or you may discover a deeper level of your feelings. In such situations, it's important to give yourself permission to come back to the person with whom you've communicated to clear things up. Also known as "going out and coming in again," this truth skill can help you deal with changing your mind, clearing up a misunderstanding, or making up after an argument. It gives you a way to continually forgive (or seek forgiveness) and begin again.

8. *Holding differences.* Holding differences refers to your ability to have your own viewpoint while at the same time being open to hearing and considering differing views. Openly listening to opposing views need not interfere with your ability to know what you feel or think about the matter. Holding differences helps you handle more complexity. You think in terms of both/and, not either/or. This practice helps you see the relationships between things that

> Holding differences helps you see the relationships between things that may appear separate or mutually exclusive.

may *appear* separate or mutually exclusive. As a result, you become much more effective in situations involving conflict, negotiation, group decision making, and problem solving. It enables you to experience the principle of mutual benefit in your relationships — the fact that any action that harms a part harms the whole and that any action that heals the collective heals the individual. I'm not going too far out on a limb to say that world peace might actually be possible if everyone on earth mastered this truth skill.

9. *Sharing mixed emotions.* When you are ambivalent, confused, or "of two minds," go ahead and express this fact. You may be pulled equally in two or more directions. Or you may feel primarily one

way (in your "foreground") but have a background feeling that's different. The ability to express complex feelings is especially useful when you are angry about what someone did but also appreciate the person's good intentions or when you want to express a strong feeling to clear up unfinished business but at the same time feel concerned about the other person's reaction. It's okay to be both angry and afraid, both resentful and appreciative, both eager and reluctant. This skill teaches you to let go of your ideas and shoulds about being consistent so that you can experience whatever shows up in your awareness.

10. *Embracing the silence.* Whenever you step fully into the present moment, you let go of the need to know how things will turn out. Your attention is on the only thing you can know — what is happening now. The most authentic response to a situation arises from a place of spaciousness, of silence, of not knowing. You can't plan everything in advance. You can't know what another person will do until she does it. If you can't tolerate not knowing and the feeling of helplessness that sometimes accompanies it, you will miss much of what is happening in the moment. Silence is your connection to the Source, the place from which new creation springs forth.

Using the Ten Truth Skills As an Awareness Practice

These ten truth skills constitute an awareness practice — a way of speaking and listening that helps you to see, accept, and deal creatively with *whatever is.* As you work with the ten skills, your ability to be present to *what is* will grow. I use the terms *whatever is* and *what is* as synonyms for what you could potentially be aware of in any given moment. Of all the sights, sounds, smells, sensations, and vibes surrounding you, how much are you able to perceive and vibrate with? You can only be as authentic as you are self-aware.

> You can only be as authentic as you are self-aware.

What is often stands in sharp contrast to what you wish were happening or think should be happening. For example, let's say a friend doesn't call when he says he will. That's what is — he said he'd call and he didn't. Do you notice what you feel? Will you listen to what he says later in explanation? Or do you interrupt your capacity to feel and to listen to your friend by immediately judging his behavior or imagining why he didn't call?

When your attention is on your mind chatter (thoughts, inferences, judgments, and interpretations), you are not present to what is happening here and now, so you cannot be real. You become more present, and therefore more real, as you peel away the layers of automatic patterns (such as judging or explaining others' behavior) and conditioned beliefs (about how safe it is to speak honestly). As you shed these layers, you will reveal your authentic self. Honest communication is the vehicle for this process. If you're being real, or relating, you might say something like, "I notice my jaw is tense. I feel angry at you for saying you'd call and then not calling." Real communication focuses on your sensations, feelings, and observations, bringing you into the present moment. This kind of communication allows for something real, unplanned, and potentially surprising and creative to occur between you and another person.

Being honest is a vital part of any awareness practice. When you express what you are honestly thinking, feeling, and wanting with the intention of relating (rather than of bolstering your position), you come to see that who you are is not defined by your thoughts, your feelings, your story, or your position. You come to experience yourself as a human being whose experience of life is constantly changing and who is okay regardless of what you feel. This profound shift in your identity is the reward for practicing Getting Real. You learn to participate in life instead of trying to control it.

> **You learn to participate in life instead of trying to control it.**

2

EXPERIENCING WHAT IS

TO GET WHERE YOU NEED TO GO, BE WHERE YOU ARE

"I'll probably see you sometime over the weekend, Mom." And with that, Mona's seventeen-year-old son Todd hopped in his car and drove off to stay at his best friend's home for the next few days. Mona's heart felt heavy as she thought, "Todd's been spending every free minute over at Jason's house. I never see him anymore. I feel so sad. And I'm jealous! He likes being at the Murphy's place better than he likes being home." Then, as her heart began to really ache, another thought entered her mind, "I shouldn't be feeling this. I should be happy that my son has good friends like the Murphys. What kind of a mother would want to possess her own son — who's almost grown-up, anyway?"

This type of ambivalence was familiar to Mona: she'd feel something and then tell herself she shouldn't be feeling it. Recognizing a pattern she didn't want to keep repeating, she decided that this time she would just let herself feel what she felt, noticing when she had the urge to cut off her feelings or talk herself out of them.

So she sat down, felt the pain in her gut, and began to cry. She sobbed out loud for about five minutes, allowing her sobs to get deeper and louder at some points and quieter at others. As she cried and felt her pain, which she thought was about the loss of her son, a memory began to emerge: it was the memory of another loss when she was about ten years old, the memory of losing her dog. Woofer had been a puppy when she got him. She had studied dog obedience training and had trained him herself to sit, roll over, heel, and beg. Then, just about the time she and Woofer were ready to attend their first dog show together, a truck struck and killed him as he was lying in the driveway just waking up from a nap. Mona was in the adjacent yard at the time and was the first one on the scene. As she held her dead dog and wailed out her pain for all to hear, her father, not realizing what had happened, yelled out the window, "Shut up, Mona. Stop being such a crybaby!"

At that moment, she stopped crying abruptly, wiped her tears on her shirt sleeve, and went in the house to tell her mother what happened. She got plenty of sympathy from everyone in the family, including her dad. But strangely, she had never cried over the incident again, until now, twenty-five years later, sitting in her kitchen feeling the "loss" of her teenage son.

When this memory came up, she started crying all over again, but now it was no longer about Todd, and she was no longer stopping herself with thoughts of "you shouldn't." She continued to sob for about ten minutes. Each wave of sobbing took her deeper into the memory. She imagined herself holding her dog in her arms and saying goodbye to him. She imagined yelling at her father, "I resent you for telling me to shut up. *You* shut up!" She comforted herself and told herself that just because her dad said to stop crying, she didn't need to obey — if this was not her truth. Dad could be pretty ignorant sometimes, she thought. And then a sense of relief and relaxation washed over her entire body. She lay down on the floor and let herself sink into the rug. As her breathing slowed and her body tingled with excitement, she felt more whole — as if a part of her that was lost had come back home for good. She saw that her current pain originated from an earlier experience of cutting off her feelings so that she wouldn't be called a cry-baby. She had never allowed herself to grieve the earlier loss, so it was still interfering with her ability to be present.

As you put yourself in Mona's place, does any of this scenario feel familiar? Do you ever start to feel something and then try to avoid feeling it? Maybe you tell yourself that the feeling is not appropriate, not reasonable, that it won't do any good, or any number of other self-suppressing messages. But as long as you avoid experiencing whatever is calling out to be

> As long as you avoid experiencing whatever is calling out to be experienced, you will not heal. A part of you will be lost.

experienced, you will not heal. A part of you will be lost. Mona allowed herself to go into what she was feeling, allowing it to reveal to her the origins of her pain about losing her son. She allowed herself to experience *what is* and discovered that self-suppression, not the current situation, was at the root of her pain. When she allowed her energy to flow naturally, expressing feelings that had been shut off long ago, she felt more relaxed and peaceful.

Practicing truth skill #1, experiencing *what is,* doesn't always look this dramatic. Sometimes we just feel irritated by something someone did or said. But any time you feel something and then notice yourself trying to avoid feeling it, it's probably more signifi-cant than it appears. Most of us are vigilant about avoiding painful feelings. So we must become equally vigilant at noticing the control patterns of our minds — because to feel what we actually feel, per-haps something that we weren't strong enough to let ourselves fully experience in the past, allows us the possibility of becoming real.

Self-Assessment Quiz

In this chapter and in the next nine, I will introduce each truth skill by asking you to take a short quiz. Each quiz is designed to help you look honestly at yourself, with reference to the truth skill covered in that chapter. The following short quiz will help you to assess your ability to experience *what is.*

On a scale from 1 to 5 (with 1 being not very much and 5 being very much), how much does each statement apply to you?

1. I often find myself thinking about what I should do or should have done.
2. I like to think of reasons for or theories about why people do what they do.
3. I have an inner critic that won't quit.
4. I often find myself comparing what I'm doing now to how things were in the past.
5. I tend to measure what's happening now against how I wish things were.
6. If I start feeling something too intensely, I have ways of cutting off those feelings.

If you scored mostly 3's, 4's, and 5's on this quiz, you probably spend a lot of time pursuing the "life of the mind." You tend to think instead of feel — to compare, judge, or theorize instead of simply experiencing *what is.* As you read this chapter, see if you can become more aware of how compulsive mental activity eclipses your ability to simply notice or feel. Remember, Getting Real does not ask that you stop using your mind — simply that you use it in the service of real creation or real survival (as opposed to the survival of your facade or act).

> Getting Real does not ask that you stop using your mind — simply that you use it in the service of real creation or real survival (as opposed to the survival of your facade or act).

Experiencing *what is* consists of two important components: the "experiencing" part and the "what is" part. Experiencing *what is* demands that you set aside your beliefs about what should or shouldn't be going on, about what you wish were going on, what you expected, what you were prepared for, what you interpret, and what

Experiencing what is also helps you make the distinction between what is, that is what you actually experience (see, hear, sense, feel, notice, remember) and what you imagine (think, interpret, evaluate, believe).

you judge as acceptable. These are all ways of maintaining an illusion of being in control. When you find yourself unable to stay with your feelings, you have an opportunity to see exactly what you're doing to avoid being present to *what is*.

What Do You "See"?

Experiencing *what is* also helps you make the distinction between *what is,* that is what you actually experience (see, hear, sense, feel, notice, remember) and what you imagine (think, interpret, evaluate, believe). Here's an example. You are driving down the highway, and another car starts to pass you on the left but then slows down and remains in the lane right next to you for a while. The driver is looking at you and laughing. What do you see? Do you see someone laughing *at you* or trying to get your attention? If so, you're making an interpretation or an inference. You see him laughing, but you do not see *why* he is laughing — you cannot see that. You can only infer, interpret, imagine, guess, or assume why. He is laughing — that's *what is*. There is a difference between *what is* and the ideas you have about it. These ideas, once again, represent an attempt to stay in control, to know something that you cannot really know. The ability to make this distinction between what you actually see and the meaning you attribute to what you see is crucial to the work of Getting Real.

Experiencing What Is in Your Relationships

Someone you care about pushes you away when you move toward her for a hug. What do you sense and feel? What do you imagine? As you answer both questions, make a clear distinction between what happened (she pushed her hand against your chest; you felt anger) and the meaning you give to this behavior (she's rejecting you). When your emotions are involved, it's often difficult to simply notice *what is* without jumping to conclusions or getting your buttons pushed.

Now imagine how you might respond to this person who has just pushed you away. Would you say:

1. Why don't you like hugging me?
2. Why are you rejecting me?
3. I resent being with someone who doesn't want to be with me.
4. I resent you for pushing me away.
5. I'm angry with you for pushing me away.
6. I feel pain about your pushing me away.
7. I'm upset by what you did, and I imagine you're losing interest in me. Are you?

Statement 1 is an example of making an assumption or jumping to a conclusion — that your friend doesn't like hugging you. In reality, all you can know is that you got pushed away. You cannot know why unless you ask. She could be simply wanting to shield you from her bad breath! Statements 2 and 3 are also both based on inferences about your friend's motives (she's rejecting you or doesn't want to be with you).

> Most couples fight about the meanings they attribute to the partner's actions.

Statements 4 through 7, on the contrary, are all based on *what is.* In statement 7, for example, by saying that you imagine she is losing interest, you are sticking to *what is* by acknowledging your imagining as just what it is — an *imagining*. Many people would say, "I think you are…" or "I feel you are…" (losing interest in me) when they really mean "I imagine you are…" Saying "I feel you are…" is confusing because you are camouflaging an interpretation or imagining as *your* feeling. Since you can only interpret, infer, or imagine what is going on inside another person, it's clearer to just say, "I imagine you are…."

As a couples counselor, I have found that most couples fight about the meanings they attribute to the partner's actions. They usually pay more attention to these meanings than to the event itself, and often they completely forget what the partner actually did in the first place. They jump to their own conclusions so fast that their ability to experience *what is* gets eclipsed. When you learn instead to simply tell others what you're feeling, without the fancy interpretations, you avoid unnecessary pain and misunderstanding.

> You don't experience an interpretation. You imagine an interpretation. And your interpretations are often a lot more painful than your actual experience.

Experiencing What Is with a Mate

For several nights in a row Joan's mate has said, "I'm too busy to spend time with you tonight." Joan had been expecting to spend time with him, and she started to imagine that the relationship is no longer important to him. She could launch into her self-protective control pattern (accusing him instead of saying what she is feeling): "Once again, you're not interested in being with me!" (said in a self-righteous tone of voice). But jumping to conclusions about her mate's behavior can only lead to unnecessary pain and misunderstanding. Joan feels hurt based on an assumption she has made, that because her mate is busy he no longer cares about her. If she were to simply experience *what is* and speak about what she feels instead of adding her own interpretation, she might still feel frustration or anger about not getting what she wants, but those feelings are quite different from the hurt arising from her interpretation about his statement. You don't *experience* an interpretation. You *imagine* an interpretation. And your interpretations are often a lot more painful than your actual experience.

If Joan were to simply tell her mate that she is angry and to say specifically what he did (saying he was too busy) that angered her without making an interpretation, then she would be making real, experiential contact with him. Her words would be far more likely to be heard and felt by him than the control-oriented pronouncement, "Once again, you're not interested..." Yet what is most important in this type of interaction is not even whether her mate hears her, but that she expresses what she really feels — as opposed to getting caught up in her "mind chatter." It is vital that she connect with what she sensed and felt when she heard her mate's actual words. In this way her expression of feeling is connected to what actually happened. If she can feel her feelings, without gumming up the works with her interpretations, she can heal or forgive. And it is generally easier for the other person to hear us nondefensively when we speak about *what* we heard them say instead of *why* we think they said it.

> Automatically responding to your worst internal fear is a common control pattern. Your buttons are pushed, and you react. This pattern keeps you in familiar emotional territory, where you don't have to risk learning anything about yourself.

If Joan automatically modifies what her mate said so that it conforms to her worst fears and then reacts to that interpretation, she will suffer unnecessarily. She'll be angry about her interpretation — not about what really happened — but will fail to notice that that's what angers her. So she won't get over it. Instead, she'll stay right where she is — hanging onto an interpretation that makes her feel wronged but righteous. The payoff for being right is that she gets to prove over and over that whenever she loves a man he winds up rejecting her. Automatically responding to your worst internal fear is a common control pattern. Your buttons are pushed, and you react. This pattern keeps you in familiar emotional territory, where you don't have to risk learning anything about yourself. You don't have to change.

Authentic contact between self and other is the aim of experiencing *what is.* And experiencing *what is* requires stepping into the unknown together in the here and now, not holding onto familiar patterns. People are much more likely to work through a conflict or misunderstanding if the conversation focuses on what both people actually experienced — and not on what they imagine the other person's actions meant. Mutual understanding will blossom when instead of trading (often very familiar) interpretations ("You never talk to me!" "Well, you only listen for what you want to hear."), partners are specific about what the other really said or did and how they really feel as a result ("You were quiet this morning, and I felt lonely.")

> People are much more likely to work through a conflict or misunderstanding if the conversation focuses on what both people actually experienced.

Experiencing versus Interpreting Exercise

We all know how easy it is to jump to conclusions about the meaning of someone's actions. We tend to interpret events in terms of what happened in the past or what could happen in the future, losing contact with the present moment. When you are able to notice your anger, hurt, resentment, and so on and see what they're about, you'll discover that, more often than not, you're responding to your interpretation rather than to what actually happened.

Try this exercise: Think of something that someone did or said that displeased you. Be specific about what was done or said. Now reflect back on the meaning or interpretation you attributed to that behavior. I recall a recent interchange between two friends of mine, Murray and Marilyn. Marilyn asked Murray to go to a social gathering with her. When he said he didn't want to go, she asked him about going to a different event in hopes that this second one might appeal to him more. What she actually said was, "Do you want to go to the Page's for dinner tonight?" and then, after he refused, "Well, how about the apple pressing party at Charlie's?" What he heard was, "You're not a good partner. You don't like to go places with me." And so they got into a fight about whether she was judging him as being a lousy partner. Obviously, one of Murray's buttons had gotten pushed. This sort of thing happens often when two people care about each other and really hate displeasing each other. Buttons make us especially sensitive to interpretations that confirm our worst fears. As you do this exercise yourself, you'll learn the most if you choose an incident that pushed your button.

> When you are able to notice your anger, hurt, resentment, and so on and see what they're about, you'll discover that, more often than not, you're responding to your interpretation rather than to what actually happened.

Now focus on something someone did that pleased you. How did you interpret their action? Someone once gave me a gift that perfectly suited my tastes. My interpretation was, "She really knows me. She really cares. She's been paying attention to what I like." That interpretation gave me a lot of pleasure. I later learned that she had bought this same gift for all the other women in our women's group. So positive experiences can be subject to misinterpretation just like negative ones can. As I reflect on this misinterpretation of mine, I can see how it is related to one of my buttons. I'm very sensitive about people giving me gifts I don't like, since this happened to me a lot at Christmas while I was growing up. Our buttons can really mess with our ability to perceive the truth of a situation. Doing this exercise will help you to experience rather than to interpret.

Noticing versus Imagining Exercise

Here is another exercise to help you learn to distinguish what you actually see, hear, or experience from what you imagine, think, or judge. In the Getting Real workshops, I ask people to pair up and tell each other something they notice about each other, and then I ask them to allow a fantasy (an imagining or interpretation) about what they see to emerge. It doesn't matter if the imaginings are correct. That's not the point. For example, one person might say, "I notice you are wearing pearls...and I imagine you're from Westchester County." Or "I notice you're tapping your finger...and I imagine you're nervous about what I'm going to say about you." Do you get the idea? Your *noticing* is usually pretty simple and undramatic. Your *imagining* can get fanciful, convoluted, and "out there." If you pay attention to your imaginings over a period of time, you may discover the same theme running

> If you pay attention to your imaginings over a period of time, you may discover the same theme running through most of them.

through most of them. For example, some people see impatience in the other person's expression whether or not the other felt impatient. Others tend to hear criticism in other people's remarks, independent of the actual circumstances.

To do this exercise, you'll need a partner. Sit face-to-face and take turns stating what you see or notice followed by what you imagine. When your partner projects an imagining onto you, don't focus on whether it's correct or not. The aim of the exercise is to consciously play with the interpretations or assessments and to consciously recognize the distinction between what your senses receive and what your mind does with this information.

A secondary aim of this exercise is to give you practice letting other people have their interpretations about you — and noticing how you feel about them. This practice helps to strengthen your inner sense of yourself — providing that you can actually allow yourself to experience what comes up in your awareness. Any time you express yourself openly, you are risking being misunderstood. It happens. This exercise helps you practice letting others think what they think. In time, you will find that even when people do misunderstand you, your sense of self is not diminished.

You can do the I notice... I imagine exercise as part of your everyday conversations with people. It's fun to practice distinguishing between what you notice and what you infer, and it shows the other person that you are not identified with your interpretation. If you say, for example, "I notice that you are looking at the floor as you talk, and I imagine you are afraid of looking me in the eye," you are owning your imagining as just that — an imagining. You are making an interpretation, but you are not saying your interpretation is right. When you take responsibility for your mind's machinations by making the distinction between what you notice and what you imagine, you help both yourself and the other person to take your interpretations more lightly.

> When you take responsibility for your mind's machinations by making the distinction between what you notice and what you imagine, you help both yourself and the other person to take your interpretations more lightly.

Playing with expressing your imaginings in this way also helps you stop projecting them onto others and gives you a feeling of being "in control" in a whole new way. As you come to identify yourself as a "noticer" instead of a "reactor," things won't push your buttons like they did before.

Other examples of mind chatter that you can learn to take more lightly are the comparisons and evaluations that often fill your inner airwaves as you move through your daily activities: "I like this, I don't like that...She's prettier, but I have a nicer figure....If I say that, he'll probably get mad." The point of experienc-

> As you come to identify yourself as a "noticer" instead of a "reactor," things won't push your buttons like they did before.

ing *what is* is to notice this behavior, not to get rid of it. Essentially, the ten truth skills will help you achieve a more spacious relationship to your internal dialogue.

A Pain in the Ego

At first, just noticing and experiencing *what is,* without embellishment, is often difficult because it's more comfortable to focus on what you think *should be* happening than on what really *is* happening. If Sara's mate leaves her for another woman, for example, she'll find it easier to focus on what he should or shouldn't have done than on her present pain. To get to the point where she can allow herself to fully experience a "pain in the ego," she'll need to learn that her ego (her mind's idea of who she is) does not solely define her. She'll need to become aware that she is also a deep and abiding presence, like the breath, that no one can damage or diminish no matter what they say or do to her.

Experiencing *what is* helps you hold your ego identity more lightly — so that you will not need to focus so much on protecting it from hurt, embarrassment, or discomfort. This truth skill brings you to an awareness of something in you, some energetic presence, that connects you to a larger reality (also called the Tao, God, Being, Life, the Force). Experiencing *what is* and expressing the feelings that arise help you stay connected to yourself, to the other person, to reality, and therefore to this larger energetic presence. For most people, disidentifying from the ego constitutes a huge shift, because we think that our ego identity is who we are. When painful memories are triggered, it can be especially difficult. Although this process can be hard work, it is the work of becoming a fully functioning human being.

> That's just another prejudice of the mind — that pain is to be avoided at all costs.

When you identify yourself primarily as your ego identity and remain unaware of your own very powerful energetic presence, you tend to believe that pain is bad. That's just another prejudice of the mind — that pain is to be avoided at all costs. To expand your capacity to experience *what is,* you'll need to be prepared to accept and welcome what's real — even if it's painful. Resisting the experience of pain can make it hurt worse. Entering it fully, as we saw from Mona's story above, can lead you through it to the other side.

Imaginary Danger

One of my teachers, Fritz Perls, used to say, "What is, is." Sounds simple, huh? But this concept is actually pretty difficult for most people to grasp. We still have to contend with our ego-minds, which have been conditioned from birth to watch out for danger. Sometimes watching for danger is appropriate, as when we look both ways before crossing a street. Too often, however, the mind imagines danger where none exists. I'll give you an example. Fern and her partner, Lance, are at a party, when Lance suddenly walks away from her. When Fern *sees* him walk away she might *imagine* he disapproves of something she did. His walking away may have nothing to do with what she imagines it's about, but her imaginings help Fern feel in control. They support the illusion that she knows what's going on. They help her anticipate what she should do to prevent further damage to her ego. In this case, for example, she can now arm herself in advance with excuses and accusations so that when she and Lance get home, she'll be prepared to defend against whatever (she imagines) he disapproved of. Such mental strategizing effectively distracts her from experiencing *what is.*

Our ego-minds are repositories for all sorts of ideas about how people are and how they should be, how things work and how they should work. Our minds do have the legitimate function of protecting us from real danger. In a potentially dangerous situation, it may serve us to have a mental model of how things worked in the past, as in: "I touched the stove burner not realizing it was still on, and I got burned. Next time I'll notice if the burner is on." But somewhere along the line in our evolution, the duties and responsibilities in the mind's job description grew beyond the mind's capabilities. So now many of us have a mind that just won't stop telling us what to watch out for, what we should or shouldn't have done, what to expect, what people are really thinking — and so much more. With all this mental noise in our perceptual field, there's very little space left over for noticing *what is* (including something that really *could* be dangerous!).

> Sometimes watching for danger is appropriate, as when we look both ways before crossing a street. Too often, however, the mind imagines danger where none exists.

Your Hero's Journey

Getting Real is a journey back to rediscovering the freshness, joy, and practicality of the simple, direct experience of each moment. It is a true hero's journey. Like the characters in ancient myths and stories, you set out on a quest (to become your real self). You meet obstacles along the way (your beliefs, judgments, shoulds, addictions, and control patterns). You get help from other people (people you share this book with, for example). You get to the top of the proverbial mountain (mastering the ten truth skills). Then, as T. S.

Eliot's famous poem "Little Gidding" describes, you arrive back where you started and "know the place for the first time."

One of the activities I ask my workshop participants to take part in is to tell a shortened version of their life story. I ask them to focus especially on incidents in which they learned how safe or unsafe it is to be truthful. Then, as we listen to each story, the audience takes note of all the beliefs, prejudices, and conclusions the speaker seems to have taken on over the course of a lifetime that interfere with simply experiencing *what is*. We infer these things both from the story itself and from the way the story is told. At the end of the exercise, after everyone has told their story, we pair up and give one another feedback about the beliefs we have identified for each person.

> Our minds do have the legitimate function of protecting us from real danger. In a potentially dangerous situation, it may serve us to have a mental model of how things worked in the past.

How Beliefs Happen

Not long ago, I was doing some management coaching with Sheldon, a thirty-five-year-old sales manager employed by a major clothing manufacturer. His story illustrates how unresolved emotional trauma can distort a person's ability to truly experience reality. Sheldon's boss, the district sales manager, had set up a series of performance coaching sessions for Sheldon because his convoluted communication style was impeding his performance. Sheldon became defensive whenever anyone asked him a direct question and therefore was not able to give clear, direct answers to questions from customers and coworkers.

One day, his manager called him in for a conference: "Hey Sheldon, I notice you haven't been calling on the O'Toole account lately. How come?" Sheldon flushed and stammered his reply: "Oh, that Richard O'Toole really lacks class. You should see the office furniture he just bought — really gaudy and tasteless. And he spends more time at the gym than at the office. I don't know about that guy." Sheldon was unaware of his manager's quizzical expression. And he had no idea how much his defensiveness was costing him until his manager recommended the coaching sessions.

Sheldon confessed to me that he had the same problem at home. His wife complained that if she'd ask him a simple question like, "Did you water the plants today?" Sheldon would get tense and tongue-tied and start making excuses: "I had to get the oil changed in my car, and I had to pick up laundry, and my boss needed me to work late."

Here is how Sheldon became aware of the roots of his defensive communication pattern. First he readily admitted that he had always been uncomfortable with any direct questioning, but he had no idea where the pattern might have originated. After he got comfortable talking about himself with me, more and more memories from his childhood began to surface. He recalled numerous instances when he was encouraged to tell the truth in response to direct questioning from his mother. When he did so, he was immediately punished. So he developed the false belief that it isn't safe to be honest, especially in response to a direct question. It soon became clear that this belief was at the root of his present defensiveness.

Sheldon told me that now, when anyone asks him a question, "It's as if there's a small, scared voice inside me, like the voice of a child, saying, 'Don't answer that. It's not safe. Watch out.'" After uncovering his outdated belief that he would get punished if he answered directly and truthfully, Sheldon decided to take some risks and test out this belief. He began, first with his wife and later with his colleagues, to stop and pay attention to his body any time he heard that little-boy voice telling him he wasn't safe. Instead of acting out his defensive pattern, he tried simply to experience all his feelings and to notice what was actually going on: his mother was nowhere in sight, and the question being asked was one he actually had an answer to. Sheldon took a few calculated risks and dared to be truthful and direct. He noticed that nothing bad happened and that things actually went pretty well. So he tried speaking honestly and directly in other situations. Soon, his defensive pattern was no longer running him. He still noticed the little voice at times, but he recognized it as a voice from the distant past.

Seeing Is Not Believing

Here's another example to further illustrate how your beliefs can impair your ability to see *what is*. Helen has a belief about how men are, which makes it difficult for her to notice exceptions to the rule. She has a preconception that men need to fix women's problems, with the result that they can't simply listen to what the women are saying. The other day when my partner asked her about her recent breakup and then asked her another question after she had finished telling him, she reacted, "There you go jumping in to fix things that can't be fixed!" He was asking her to elaborate on something that had piqued his sincere interest, but as soon as he opened his mouth, she immediately jumped to the conclusion that he was trying to fix her. Helen's belief that men only want to fix her feelings was a powerful button for her, so when it gets pushed, she becomes automatically defensive or aggressive.

> A button is a "belief gone mad."

I introduced the notion of buttons earlier. A button is a "belief gone mad." It is a predisposition to feel hurt, slighted, or attacked when you imagine that your negative expectations have been fulfilled. If you believe that people see you as unable to take care of yourself, your button will get pushed and you'll overreact when someone tries to open the car door for you. Or if you fear that whenever you get close to people, they leave you, then you'll overreact when your partner wants some time alone.

You can learn to slow down your reaction time once you have identified your buttons and beliefs. Just becoming aware of how your beliefs cloud your vision can go a long way toward helping you take the time to find out what is really going on, as in: "I feel myself contracting and starting to get defensive. I want you to tell me what you meant when you said that." Once you have tried testing reality a few times and found out something that you didn't know (relating), you will learn that it actually feels better than pretending or assuming that you already know (controlling).

Noticing What's Happening Exercise

Once you have begun to detach from your identification with your beliefs and judgments, you will be in better shape to notice what you are actually experiencing in the present moment.

Find a friend who will be willing to do this exercise with you: Sit facing each other. Take turns saying out loud what you sense or notice in your body: "I notice (or I am aware of) my breath going in and out of my nostrils." "I notice a tingling sensation in my genitals." "I notice tension in my jaw." Then do a round of sharing what you notice in the room: "I notice the sunlight coming in through the window." "I notice the movement of the clouds outside." "I notice a dark stain on the rug." If you wish, you can stop reading and do this by yourself right now. Relax and pay attention to what you notice in your body. See if you can simply notice first the sensations in your body and then the things you observe in your surroundings, without judging them as good or bad, significant or insignificant.

> Once you have begun to detach from your identification with your beliefs and judgments, you will be in better shape to notice what you are actually experiencing in the present moment.

In my workshops, we then go around the circle and share what we notice happening in our minds. Usually we share what we notice ourselves saying inwardly in the moment, what I call "self-talk": "I'm saying to myself I hope the group is impressed by what I just shared"; "I notice I'm judging Tony, thinking he should be paying attention"; "I'm thinking that I should have something more significant to say."

Again, stop reading for a minute, and pay attention to what you are saying to yourself in this moment. There is no correct thing that you should or shouldn't be saying. Most people have an internal commentary going on all the time. "I shouldn't be taking so much time with this." "After this, I'm going to get something to eat." "This is a waste of time."

> The mind likes to compare our present state with some wished-for and often unattainable state. It likes to aspire to being "better" (which is often a control pattern to avoid experiencing how you really are).

These awareness exercises are simple but not easy for many of us. Our active minds have trouble being satisfied with just the facts. The mind likes to compare our present state with some wished-for and often unattainable state. It likes to aspire to being "better" (which is often a control pattern to avoid experiencing how you really are). And it likes to attach significance to what we perceive.

Your Real Self Doesn't Need Protecting

As I have noted, your mental chatter is simply the mind's attempt to protect itself — to avoid the anxiety or helplessness of not knowing or not being in control. Yet your real self, your presence, you as the noticer, doesn't need protecting or defending. It simply needs to be experienced. The more you experience yourself as "the one who notices," the safer you will feel. My mother often used to remind me, "No one can take anything away from you if it really belongs to you." As you proceed on your hero's journey, you will learn to distinguish between what really belongs to you (your presence or beingness) and what is nonessential or transitory (your ideas about yourself).

In the following chapters, you will learn how the nine other truth skills relate to this first one. Experiencing *what is* is the foundation on which the other truth skills rest. You won't be able to pick up these other skills until you have some ability to distinguish *what is* from your judgments and assessments. Likewise, the more you practice the other truth skills, the greater will be your capacity to experience *what is*.

Experiencing What Is in a Nutshell

- Experiencing *what is* means allowing yourself to feel what you feel without inhibiting yourself shutting down.
- If you discover that you are inhibiting yourself, notice this. And if you feel pain about it, feel the pain. Allow the noticing of the pain to guide you to whatever shows up next in your awareness, and experience that.
- Eventually, by experiencing whatever comes up in your awareness, you will be able to confront your energy blocks, your control patterns, and your false beliefs and to move through them to a place of healing. If you cannot experience *what is,* it will be impossible to heal.
- Learn to make the crucial distinction between what you notice or experience and what you judge, assess, interpret, or believe. Don't let your ego-mind take you on its trip!
- Experiencing *what is* requires that you be willing to step into the unknown. You cannot control where your experiencing will take you.
- Notice and report your sensations, your feelings, your thoughts, your judgments, and your self-talk. Share these

honestly as a way to move past them to whatever calls your attention next.

- The object of experiencing and expressing is to keep yourself engaged in the flow of life, to experience yourself as a cocreative participant in this big evolutionary dance we call life. Doing so will help you to avoid taking any one interaction too seriously.

BEING TRANSPARENT

3

FREEDOM'S JUST ANOTHER WORD FOR NOTHING LEFT TO HIDE

Jenny and Fred were having a dinner party for a few other couples to celebrate their thirtieth wedding anniversary. A lovely bottle of champagne was being poured, and it was time for toasts. Fred lifted his glass, first to the guests and then to his smiling wife: "I tried to do research on the Internet for something inspiring having to do with thirty years, but all I could find was a reference to the Thirty Years War...." At that point one of the other guests, trying to rescue Fred, interrupted the toast with another attempt at humor, so Fred never got to complete his thought. He was planning to talk about how rewarding his life with Jenny had been in spite of a few skirmishes here and there, but he never got a chance to say what he'd planned. All Jenny could think was, "He compares our marriage to the Thirty Years War!" She felt hurt and had a hard time making eye contact with Fred. As she sat there stunned, trying to be a good sport and enjoy her dinner, she realized she had a couple of options: she could ignore her feelings and fake it for the rest of the party or she could speak about her feelings. She decided to speak up: "Fred, I'm sitting here trying to tell myself that your comment comparing our marriage to the Thirty Years War was nothing to be upset by, but

I'm noticing my heart is pounding, and I'm having trouble making eye contact with you. I don't want to carry this feeling for the entire evening. So, in spite of the fact that this is a formal dinner party, I want to say I do feel very upset and angry, and I hope you can understand why."

A hush went over the couple's elegant dining room, as the guests waited for Fred's response. After a brief pause, Fred, looking flustered and embarrassed, did reply: "Hey, I'm feeling really awful too! I feel how that must've come across to you, Jenny, but I didn't get to finish my toast. I was going to say that in spite of our occasional skirmishes, we've had a pretty wonderful life all these thirty years. I'm so sorry that hurt you." The guests heaved a collective sigh of relief as Jenny gave Fred a warm smile and said, "Wow, I feel better now. Thanks, Fred. Thanks, everyone."

> When you're letting someone know how his words affected you, it's important to be specific about what you heard.

If you had been in Jenny's situation, what would you have done? Can you picture yourself taking the risk of making your guests uncomfortable to express yourself and clear the air? Or would you have sat on your feelings, hoping they'd go away, and maybe tell Fred later? Or would you have chastised yourself for being too sensitive and try to get over it? Or perhaps you'd have simply told yourself that it was no big deal.

The choice you make reflects your beliefs about how safe it is to be honest, to let yourself be seen by others. Noticing your choices in such situations and experiencing your feelings as you take action is what Getting Real is about. Then you make the choice either to let yourself be seen or to hide, pretend, withhold, or talk yourself out of your feelings (as in, "it's no big deal"). Noticing and becoming aware are the work of truth skill #1, experiencing *what is.* Expressing what you feel or notice is the domain of truth skill #2, the subject of this chapter.

Jenny's statement to Fred was motivated by an attempt to clear the air so she could get over her hurt and anger and enjoy the rest of the party. It came from her intent to know and be known (to relate), not to make Fred feel bad or look bad in front of their guests (to control). When you communicate with the intent to relate, you will naturally become more transparent, that is, easier to know. You aren't being strategic or trying to manipulate the outcome. You're being open and sincere, with no hidden agenda. You'll learn more about relating and controlling in chapter 4, "Noticing Your Intent."

Note that Jenny also spoke about what she observed in her body — that her heart was pounding and that she was having trouble making eye contact with her husband. Here she was using truth skill #1, experiencing

> Being specific helps you connect to your felt experience instead of to your interpretation.

what is. And she was specific about what Fred did that angered her. When you're letting someone know how his words affected you, it's important to be specific about what you heard. Jenny did include one gross inaccuracy however, which made her statement less effective than it might have been: she assumed that Fred was comparing their marriage to the Thirty Years War, when actually, according to Fred, that was not what he was doing at all. So if Jenny had said, "I heard you say 'Thirty Years War,' and I assumed you were comparing our marriage to that," that would have been more effective.

Some people in Fred's place would have immediately gotten defensive if they heard their wife misinterpret their behavior as Jenny did. So if you can, repeat back exactly what the other said that offended you. That way you're both working off the same reality blueprint. Also, being specific helps you connect to your felt experience instead of to your interpretation. When you replay the words, you can more readily return to exactly what you were experiencing when you heard them. But whatever words you use, the point is to notice what you are doing. The ten truth skills that you are learning constitute a way of using language that fosters clearer noticing, deepening self-awareness, and more open contact between people.

Self-Assessment Quiz

Here's another quiz. Give yourself a 1 to 5 rating for each item (with 1 being usually not true of you and 5 being mostly true).

1. I have trouble openly expressing my emotions.
2. I have trouble telling my sexual partner what I like and desire most.
3. I have trouble saying things that I think will hurt someone's feelings or upset them.
4. I have trouble showing weakness, vulnerability, or uncertainty.
5. I have trouble revealing things I've done that I'm ashamed of.
6. I have difficulty telling someone when I'm sexually attracted to him or her.
7. I fear that I would scare people away if they knew what I really felt.

How many 3's, 4's, and 5's did you give yourself? If you got some, you've made a good start on acknowledging and accepting your fears about being transparent in certain situations.

Let's examine some of those situations. Are you able to reveal certain things about yourself with strangers more than with loved ones? Do you have an easier time with anger than with softer feelings, or vice versa? Do you lie or withhold mostly to ensure getting what you want? Or do you try to hide the fact that you have wants? Is sex a challenging

> The first and most important part of being transparent is seeing yourself without praise or blame.

arena for you? Or do you have more insecurities regarding your competence at work? Do you worry about hurting people? Do you worry about getting hurt? Do you mostly lie to *yourself* so you won't feel the pain of your situation or so you won't have to confront others?

If you can answer these questions honestly, you are being transparent right now, at least with yourself. As you consider these questions, what do you notice? What do you sense in your body? What feelings do you have? What is your self-talk? Are you aware of any theories or judgments? The first and most important part of being transparent is seeing yourself without praise or blame. Seeing yourself is an act of observation, not of evaluation. This practice requires a level of competence with truth skill #1. The reason most people give for not being transparent is that they experience a gap between how they are and how they think they should be. Then they beat themselves up about the disparity and try to at least look like how they think they should be. But now

> Any time you feel unsafe or unable to be honest about yourself, it means you have energy tied up in a false belief, probably unconscious, that is still dictating your life choices.

instead of realizing that their pain is about living a pretense, they think their pain is about not being "better."

Let's go back to the questions about the situations in which you have trouble being truthful. Any time you feel unsafe or unable to be honest about yourself, it means you have energy tied up in a false belief, probably unconscious, that is still dictating your life choices. If it's hard for you to express anger or displeasure, for example, you may harbor the belief that if you express such feelings you will be punished. In the introduction, I shared my fear of expressing anger to someone who is already angry with me. That fear originated when I talked back to my father and he slapped me across the mouth. In psychology, we call that "one-trial learning." Although an incident might happen only once, it can still leave a powerful imprint on the ego, that part of the mind designed to protect and defend us against danger. An enduring false belief is often the result of this type of event. I call this type of learning "learning the wrong thing." The mind, in its overzealous efforts to protect the being that you are, generalizes the learning from one incident to all incidents that it finds similar.

The work of Getting Real involves using the ten truth skills to notice evidence of and then reveal to your consciousness all the times you learned the wrong thing. Then you can reevaluate your mind's generalized fear in light of actual current circumstances. Let's say, for example, that when you expressed anger as a child, someone told you that if you want people to like you, you shouldn't be angry, that anger was ugly. Maybe at that time you really believed you needed everyone to like you or to find you attractive. But as you have grown up, you have probably noticed that the cost to your self-respect of trying to please everyone is enormous. So now you can reevaluate your no-anger policy in light of your present reality. Noticing when you have trouble being transparent is a big step.

Getting Real in Dating

Kevin, a frequent participant in my groups, submitted a personal ad to the Meet Your Mate section of his local newspaper. In the ad he described himself as financially successful, when in reality he is a single parent struggling to support his family, has no savings, and experiences a great deal of anxiety about his financial situation. After the ad was published, Kevin hardly recognized himself when he read it, and he realized that he was not able to be transparent about his finances. What was the should or false belief that was running him? he wondered. He first took an honest look at his present situation in an effort to simply experience *what is*. He recalled his most recent financial interactions with friends, customers, and his teenage children. He noticed a tight feeling in his chest and some shaming self-talk. Kevin got a clear picture of his present financial situation and just let himself look at this picture as soberly as possible, without denial or blame.

Then he paid closer attention to the tight feeling in his chest. As he stayed with the experience of tightness, it became a sharp pain near his heart. The pain got more intense, and he feared he might be having a heart attack. This fear went away after he noticed and accepted it rather than working himself into a sweat over it. As he continued to focus on the pain (instead of either dramatizing it or denying it, as he was wont to do), he got a mental picture of a past incident in his life. He was about eight years old. His parents and he were all huddled behind the living room couch in their working-class home in north Philadelphia. What was going on? Who were we hiding from? Then, in his vision, he heard a loud and persistent knocking at the front door. It was a bill collector — someone hired to collect money from his father for the various debts he owed. Kevin noticed an ache in his heart for what he imagined was his dad's pain and shame about the situation. His dad was holding his left hand, and Kevin could feel all the tension from his father's body entering his left side, right into his heart.

As Kevin stayed with his pain and the imagery it produced, he began to sob. He sobbed for what seemed like a long time, but he later realized it had only been about five minutes. While he was sobbing, he felt himself grow bigger and let go of his dad's hand. He experienced sorrow for his dad, then a growing sense of detachment. When anger at his dad came up, he let himself feel that too. And finally, Kevin saw the situation from a broader perspective. He could see the whole scene: his mom, his dad, and him as a boy doing what they felt they needed to do at the time. He felt compassion for the three of them. He even felt some compassion for the faceless, nameless bill collector. Then he sat down at his desk and rewrote his personal ad. Now he included in his ad the words "struggling to achieve financial sobriety." Not long after this ad was printed, he met a woman who eventually became a good friend. She also had unresolved money issues. Through what he had learned about himself, through honestly looking at and experiencing his pain, and then through becoming more transparent, he was able to assist his new friend in achieving a more sober relationship to money.

Secrets and Lies

Another good way to let go of unconscious beliefs and to see yourself more honestly is to examine the secrets you keep from others. I have never met anyone who doesn't have secrets. But consider this: the fact that you have secrets is the same thing as affirming, "If people really knew me, they wouldn't accept me" (translation: "I'm not acceptable as I am"). We knock ourselves out to appear acceptable by doing things that reinforce the feeling that we are not. What secrets do you have? What things have you done (or thought) that you wouldn't want anyone to know about? If you can let yourself look at your secrets, you can learn from them. In some of my workshops I do a Secrets Exercise, in which I pass out blank three-by-five cards and ask people to anonymously write one of their secrets on a card. Then I collect the cards, shuffle them, and pass them out again. All the participants read aloud their new card (probably not their own secret) as if it were theirs. They attempt to feel what it might feel like if this secret belonged to them. They then talk about what it feels like to have this secret, to have done, said, or thought whatever had been reported on the card. This exercise provides a healing experience for everyone in the room. As you hear your secret read aloud and

> We knock ourselves out to appear acceptable by doing things that reinforce the feeling that we are not.

discussed by someone else in such a tender, intimate way, you see your secret in a fresh light. Your secret, the thing you thought too terrible to reveal, starts to seem more normal. In

Perhaps they know intuitively that if others could hear and possibly accept their secrets, they would be provided with some measure of reassurance or healing.

fact, the depth of self-disclosure in this exercise sometimes amazes the participants. It's as if people are actually dying to unburden their darkest secrets. Perhaps they know intuitively that if others could hear and possibly accept their secrets, they would be provided with some measure of reassurance or healing.

In one of my groups, a man of about fifty shared a very painful secret, first anonymously on the card, and then openly by claiming the secret as his after it had been read and discussed. His secret was that he felt responsible for killing his best friend when they were in the seventh grade. Smitty, the man in my group, and his two friends, John and Brian, his very best friends since kindergarten, had taken Smitty's dad's handgun to the golf course one day to play around. Hoping to impress his friends with his bravery, Smitty got the idea of playing Russian roulette. The others, especially Brian, protested, saying it was a stupid idea. But Smitty persisted and somehow got his friends to agree. Smitty loaded one chamber of the pistol and volunteered to go first. He spun the barrel, put the gun to his temple, closed his eyes tightly, and pulled the trigger. Click. Nothing happened. He was lucky. Feeling a bit more confident, Brian took his turn next. But this time, when he pulled the trigger, it went off, killing him instantly. All these details were not written on the card. All Smitty had written on the card was, "I am responsible for someone's death." But after he heard the person read the card with such heartfelt remorse and with such compassion, Smitty decided to speak up. He told the entire story with tears streaming down his face. When he finished, a hush went over the group. Several other group members were crying with him. As Smitty looked around, his sobs got deeper. He cried out to his dear friend's memory, asking for forgiveness. In subsequent group sessions, we learned that this confession was a life-changing healing experience for Smitty. He had allowed his most shameful secret to be seen and had experienced love instead of the contempt he expected.

Being Transparent Exercise

Here is an exercise you can do alone to help you become more transparent. On four different cards, write the names of four people you respect. Now shuffle the cards and turn them over. On the other side of each of the cards, write your top four secrets. Shuffle the cards again. Read each card in turn, starting with the person's name, then turning the card over and reading the secret. If the secret belonged to this person, how would that change your opinion of him or her? If you're saying to yourself that it wouldn't change your opinion at all, notice that. If it would, notice that too. Can you accept other peoples' dark secrets more easily than your own? Or is it the other way around?

> He had allowed his most shameful secret to be seen and had experienced love instead of the contempt he expected.

Now pick one of the secrets you have written and feel your feelings associated with it. If it's a memory of something you have done, feel the feelings you have about having done it. As you go into the feeling, notice any tendency you may have to run away from it. Notice any judgments or imaginings, then come back to the feelings. If they take you into a memory, stay with this memory. If not, simply feel what you feel. Either way, by experiencing *what is,* you allow light to shine on one of the dark places in your psyche, allowing this dark place to be integrated into the whole of your being. Once integrated, it won't have any hidden power over you.

Favorite Fears

Everyone lies, everyone has secrets, and everyone has fears, so there's no point in admonishing people to stop it. What works better, what helps us to become more transparent, is to admit our fears and to name them. Most people have one or two "favorite fears." Some of us tend to fear being ignored; others fear being singled out for attention. Some of us fear abandonment; others fear being smothered. Some fear being overwhelmed or overstimulated, others avoid emptiness or having nothing to do. Frequently your favorite fear only emerges in certain types of situations.

To help you get perspective on your fears and take them more lightly, look at the following list of situations and put a 0, 1, 2, or 3 next to each one, 0 meaning you're confident and self-trusting in this situation, 1 meaning you'd be moderately shaky or unsure of yourself in this situation, 2 meaning you'd prefer to avoid it, and 3 meaning you hope never to be faced with this situation. Then, after you have given each situation a rating, go down the list again and wherever you have put a 1, 2, or 3 ask yourself, What do I imagine would happen to me if I were in this situation? What specifically am I afraid of?

> Everyone lies, everyone has secrets, and everyone has fears, so there's no point in admonishing people to stop it.

1. Telling a lover I don't like what they are doing to pleasure me.
2. Being told my lover isn't happy with something I'm doing during lovemaking.
3. Telling an employee or coworker that I'm not satisfied with something they have done.
4. Being told by a boss, coworker, or customer that they are unhappy with my work.
5. Starting a conversation with someone I'm attracted to.

6. Having someone whom I'm not attracted to ask me to accompany them to a party.

7. Walking into a gathering full of people and doing something unusual, unexpected, or foolish that makes everyone notice me.

8. Walking into a gathering full of people and having no one notice me.

9. Being asked to do an assignment at work that I think is beyond my capabilities.

10. Having to give a performance review to someone I detest or don't respect.

11. Being caught in a lie.

12. Being blamed for something I didn't do.

13. Expressing a tender feeling and being misunderstood.

14. Being told that I'm not good at something that I want to be good at.

15. Having my boss tell me she is angry with me.

16. Having a customer tell me he is angry with me.

17. Having someone tell me I have done something that hurt her feelings.

18. Telling someone he has done something that I feel hurt about.

19. Telling someone he has done something that angers me.

20. Telling someone "it's over between us."

21. Negotiating for what I want with someone who is behaving in a dominating, threatening manner.

22. Telling someone she has to leave my home or office.

23. Being told by someone that he wants me to leave.

24. Shedding tears in a group meeting.

25. Having a temporary physical condition that makes it necessary for me to ask for help.

26. Being asked for help with some physical task.

27. Being asked for nurturance.

28. Being told to calm down or to not be emotional.

29. Being told to shut up.

30. Hearing a negative judgment about myself.

31. Letting someone know my judgments about her.

32. Being told by someone I like that he doesn't like something about my personality.

33. Telling a friend or mate that I want to be treated a certain way and having her refuse.

34. Wanting my friend or mate to pay attention to me and being ignored.

35. Being told to do something that I don't want to do by someone whose approval I seek.

36. Being told I'm wrong about something I feel strongly about.

Know Fear

Getting familiar with your fears can help you to take them more lightly. Many people suffer unnecessarily because they try to hide what they're afraid of. If you accept your fears, they won't rule your behavior as much as if you try to pretend they don't exist. The exercise you just did was to help you identify the things you imagine could happen to you in certain situations that may be fear provoking to you. Being specific about what you fear helps to eliminate the kind of generalized anxiety that many people live with every day. Often, when you attempt to name what you specifically fear, you realize that your fear is without substance. You discover that your fear is an imagining — probably related to a false belief that originated when you were at a much more vulnerable stage of life.

If you do have a specific fear that feels powerful and real, take the time to acknowledge it so you can feel it fully, get down to the false belief that may lie beneath it, and clear it out of your system. Perhaps you will discover a desire underneath the fear. Since expressing a desire takes more emotional strength and courage than expressing a fear, many people tend to express their fears as a "sideways" method of asking for what they want. For example, Jean tells her co-worker Tara that she is afraid to ask for Tara's help with her project. She imagines that Tara is too busy. When Jean checks in with herself to discover what she specifically fears, she finds it's about being told no. Once she admits this, she is able to see the want underneath the fear.

> Often, when you attempt to name what you specifically fear, you realize that your fear is without substance.

Now she can say to Tara, "I'd like your input on this project." After acknowledging the fear of being told no, she realized that hearing no is not so scary after all. It was more frightening when it was a vague sense of dread. Now that Jean has named the fear, it doesn't seem so serious and she can let go of it and simply express what she wants.

Remember, when you try to ignore your fear and push it into the background, it won't go away. Instead, it will either create confusion in your perception of what's true or it will lead to a lack of authenticity in the way you express yourself. So if authenticity is your goal, acknowledge your fear, clarify what it's about, and let it fade away.

Being Transparent in Marriage

If your mate just bought you an expensive birthday gift but it's something you don't like and will probably never use, what would you do? You might be afraid of appearing unappreciative or of hurting your mate's feelings. Yet you probably won't be able to successfully hide your true feelings. I suggest you think of your dilemma as an opportunity to be transparent, to show your vulnerability (which means your ability to be affected by things). You might say, "Darling, I have been afraid to tell you this...I feel shaky in my body as I speak...but I want to be completely transparent with you. I appreciate you for getting me such a generous gift. And at the same time I want to let you know that it's not my taste. I want us to be completely honest

> If you do have a specific fear that feels powerful and real, take the time to acknowledge it so you can feel it fully, get down to the false belief that may lie beneath it, and clear it out of your system.

with each other, even if it's painful sometimes."

You may be thinking to yourself, "That is a fairly good way to say it, but I don't think on my feet that fast." Well, neither do most people. So in real time, you might hide your true feelings at first and then have to come back to your mate later and come clean. (Chapter 8 covers this topic in depth.) That's the best most of us can do when we're first starting out with Getting Real. That's okay. Being transparent doesn't mean being perfect or polished in your honesty. It means showing yourself, warts and all.

The Freedom to Screw Up

Now let's consider the connection between fear and freedom. As the subtitle of this chapter states, freedom's just another word for nothing left to hide. As long as you have something you can't let yourself or others see, you're limiting your freedom. I'm not telling you to share everything that comes into your mind. But if you are not able to express something, if you are compelled to keep it hidden, then you are not free to choose an authentic response to each situation.

Revealing your truth is a discovery process. Sometimes you'll take a risk and disclose something and then realize it was not what you meant or that it doesn't represent how you now feel. It may have seemed true at the time, but now you see something you didn't see before, or maybe your feelings have changed. That's why it's a good idea to create a support system for yourself in your effort to become more transparent. You need people who will give you a second chance when you screw up — who will allow you to "go out and come in again," as chapter 8 describes. You need people around you who agree to Get Real together. You need people who want to know you and to know themselves — people who place a higher value on relating than on controlling.

> As long as you have something you can't let yourself or others see, you're limiting your freedom.

My partner and I have a way of making all truths feel safe. If we imagine that something may be difficult for the other to hear, we begin our disclosure with the words, "In the interest of transparency...." This phrase signals a benevolent intent, even if the information is hard to take in. When you preface your anger or resentment this way, it helps you stay connected to the intent "to know and be known," to share information about you and your feelings, and it keeps you from sliding into using your self-expressions as punishment or as a way to control. Mainly, though, it helps you manage your own fears about the disclosure. Once it becomes understood between you and another person that all disclosures, even anger and disappointment, are in the interest of transparency, the preamble will no longer be needed. I think of this phrase as the training wheels you can use while you are learning to speak and deliver difficult truths.

Creating Real Community

Getting Real is a process to be shared with like-minded others. We learn to accept our own dark or hidden aspects by first disclosing them to others and then feeling their acceptance. Acceptance does not equal approval or agreement but rather a willingness to stay engaged. You'll need to find people who value learning to hear truth more than they value being comfortable. This may seem impossible as you look around at your circle of friends. That's why I created the Getting Real Card Game as a companion to this book. (See appendix C for a description and ordering information.) Just about everyone can enjoy the game — without committing themselves to any particular level of self-disclosure. You may be surprised to learn that people you never thought of as emotionally courageous are actually quite ready to Get Real when they feel permission to do so.

Who Are You Protecting?

Many people experience fear only when certain "taboo" thoughts or emotions come up — such as anger, judgmental thoughts, or emotional or sexual hunger. Most of us learned the "right" way to express "unacceptable" thoughts or emotions a long time ago. In most cases, "right" meant without making a mess or without making other people uncomfortable. When we were little, our parents probably became uncomfortable (or worse) when we complained, threw fits, played with ourselves, or couldn't be satisfied, so we learned to keep the lid on these things. We learned either to pro-

> We continue to believe we can protect people by avoiding anything we imagine would make them uncomfortable.

tect others from feeling uncomfortable or to protect ourselves from their reactions to us. As adults we continue protecting people. We continue to believe we can protect people by avoiding anything we imagine would make them uncomfortable. Thus, we confuse their discomfort zone with our own, as we try to protect them at the cost of our own well-being.

What do you believe would happen if you stopped trying to protect others? What could another person do to you? How could he or she hurt you? Let's look at the beliefs and baggage you carry around about your ability to handle strong feelings. Let's open some of those old bags to see what's inside. When I have asked workshop participants to do this, here are some of the things they have said:

"My mom hit me whenever I talked back. I'm still afraid of being hit — even though that seems ridiculous to me in this moment."

"I think my mom withdrew from me when I cried too much. I think it made her feel like a bad mother. So now I imagine that if I'm not satisfied in sex, my partner will withdraw."

"My mom criticized me when I called attention to myself. Now I'm afraid to show it when I'm feeling really needy for affection or attention. I try to remain pretty much invisible."

"My dad flew off the handle a lot, and my mom thought he was a jerk. So now I think if I show anger, people will judge me as a jerk."

"When I got really exuberant as a little kid, my dad mocked me. He made fun of me. I got the idea that being happy and joyful meant you were stupid."

If you are like most people, you probably have a story about how you arrived at the beliefs you now hold. Everyone I know has a past that clouds their perception of the truth. Where anger, sex, neediness, and joy are concerned, people need a lot of help from their friends to Get Real. We can't underestimate how strongly we've been socialized into suppressing ourselves. We need supportive others to provide us with what psychotherapists call "a corrective emotional experience," an experience of someone we care about receiving our uninhibited expression of feelings with acceptance.

The Unfinished Business Exercise

One of the most liberating and energizing exercises we do in the Getting Real workshop is the unfinished business exercise. Each person picks a partner who will take on the role of someone in their past from whom they have withheld significant feelings in the area of anger, sex, or desires. Usually we work on withheld anger first. If you are my partner, I sit facing you and allow my feelings to come to the surface. Then I let my anger and resentments fly, using the phrase "I resent you for_____"(followed by something specific that this person did, said, or did not do). The other person is instructed to be as neutral as possible so as to be a good projection screen.

I ask people to do each round for at least five minutes. If they run out of withheld emotions, they can repeat themselves. In fact, they are encouraged to repeat themselves when the feeling is especially strong. At the end of this exercise, people are laughing and crying and hugging one another and jumping up and down. They're like little kids again — open, free, spontaneous. What has happened? They report feelings like: "I let her have it, and the roof didn't cave in! I'm still here." "I didn't know I had that much juice bottled up in me! Wow!" "I was really angry, and I could also feel love and compassion once I got the anger out."

It seems that people are dying to "let it all hang out" — especially when taboo feelings are concerned. They just need permission to do so. Of course, there aren't a lot of settings in which this permission exists in most people's daily lives. But you can build this support into your life. If your experience is anything like mine, you will find that meeting regularly with a group of people who value Getting Real will give you the courage you need to be yourself, even beyond the safety of the group setting. For several years now, I have been hosting a monthly practice group for people who have taken my one-day Getting Real workshop. We're all finding that the more we practice expressing taboo thoughts and feelings with one another, the more authentic and confident we become in the rest of our lives. Group members report being more real with their parents, bosses, coworkers, and mates.

The Resentments/Appreciations Clearing Practice

I teach a number of clearing rituals that support people being transparent with one another. Ritualizing honest communication, that is setting aside a special time and place for expressing withheld feelings, makes everything feel safer. People are more likely to view a ritual as an awareness and clearing practice rather than as a threat. The most popular clearing ritual is the Gestalt therapy exercise of sharing resentments and appreciations.

To do the practice, you'll need one or more people who agree to be your practice partner(s). Ask them to read this book so they can understand the rationale for the regular sharing of resentments and appreciations. If you are in a relationship, your mate would be the ideal person to do it with. In the following section, I have reprinted the guidelines I offer to couples in my Relating More, Controlling Less couples workshops. If you are not part of a couple, you can adapt this material to fit your situation.

Suggestions for Your Regular "R and A" Practice

1. Decide together how often you will do the ritual: every day, every other day, weekly, and so on.

2. Choose one member of the couple to initiate the process (as in, "When is a good time to do our resentments and appreciations? Is now a good time?") Take turns being the initiator, one week at a time.

3. Designate a safe, sacred space for the ritual by choosing a place in your home or yard where you will be uninterrupted and where you can sit facing each other. It's helpful to do the ritual in the same place every time you do it. That way when you walk into this room or area, you have the sense that you are entering a different mind-set — a mind-set in which you set aside any need to prove your point or bolster your position. Your aim is transparency — to know and be

known. Revealing resentments is an act of making yourself vulnerable. We may fear that our resentments will appear self-ish or petty or unenlightened and that it's a risk to reveal them. Some people like to sanctify the space by doing something like lighting a candle, smudging, or burning incense.

4. Decide on time limits for each person's turn. You can take less time than your limit, but not more.

5. When it is the other person's turn, don't interrupt (except if you need to remind them to be more specific. Then ask, "Can you be specific?").

6. Use the words "I resent/appreciate you for_____" (and be specific about what the other did, said, or did not do).

7. If your partner is making an interpretation without giving you the data this is based on ask, "Can you be specific?" This is a signal for the partner to recognize that she or he is imagining or interpreting. It also gives you the time to get centered so that you'll be less apt to overreact.

8. If after trying, you can't be specific, then use a phrase like: "I resent you for what I interpret (or imagine) as your inability to hear my anger." (Better still would be: "I resent you for not looking at me and for moving away from me when I expressed my anger.")

9. Speak only about what you experienced: what you saw, heard, sensed, or felt. If you must base your resentment or appreciation on an interpretation or imagining, okay; but try first to see if you can recall something specific that happened. Usually people find it easiest to state what was not done, as in "I resent you for not telling me you appreciate the back rub I gave you." This signals that you had an expectation that was disappointed and that you're taking responsibility for it. Try not to limit yourself to these kinds of resentments, because your partner actually did do something that triggered the resentment.

10. At the end of the process, share something that you appreciate about yourself. And end it by appreciating each other for engaging in the practice.

I suggest using this form for several reasons. First, saying "I" helps keep you grounded in your own experience. Second, using an "I . . . you" sentence helps you feel the connection between you and the other person. It helps train you to not be afraid of giving or receiving strong contact, and it helps you not lose yourself in the face of strong contact. The ability to make strong contact is a prerequisite for intimacy. Third, stating what the other specifically did or didn't do helps create a felt sense in your body, helping you to move through your feelings and past them to forgiveness.

> The ability to make strong contact is a prerequisite for intimacy.

Being specific also eliminates the temptation to argue over conflicting interpretations. It helps keep you focused on one person's actual memory of what happened rather than on that person's interpretation. Being specific is harder for some people than for others, but it will get easier as you feel safer doing the practice. Even if you can only partially recall the specifics, they are still helpful. Don't get perfectionistic about it.

Please do not assume that when your partner only gives you a few specific details that these details represent the full picture of what he or she is resenting or appreciating. In other words, don't expect complete accuracy of detail. If your partner can only remember part of what you said or did, try not to let your "I'm being misunderstood" button get pushed. See if you can be spacious enough to allow the other to have feelings, even if they cause you pain or upset. Just notice your upset and the thoughts and feelings associated with it. You can express this as a resentment when it's your turn.

Fourth, even appreciations are to be gotten over so that you can detach from your ideas about what things mean and stay open to *what is.* Spiritual freedom comes from participating in the moment-by-moment flow of life, not by getting things to be just right once and for all. Fifth, this clearing ritual is an awareness practice as well as a communication tool. It helps you develop a more spacious, less reactive consciousness. It helps you continually clear away old unfinished business so you can be present to what is actually going on. It helps free you from the need to control how others view you. It helps you get over feeling responsible for another's feelings. It teaches you that you can listen to viewpoints that differ from yours without losing your own. It helps you trust yourself in facing the unknown.

And last, the "I . . . you" form does not imply that the other is responsible for your feelings. You can resent someone for something she did without holding the belief that she did something wrong or caused your reaction or that you are right. A feeling is just a feeling — neither right nor wrong. And only you know what your feelings are. Refrain from telling the other about him- or herself. Talk about *yourself.* The R and A clearing ritual can be used with anyone you're close to or would like to feel closer to. Many people discover that after doing it with their parents(s), what had been a lifeless or strained relationship comes alive again.

> Spiritual freedom comes from participating in the moment-by-moment flow of life, not by getting things to be just right once and for all.

Being Transparent with a Parent

Remember Smitty, the man who felt responsible for the death of his best friend? In our workshop, Smitty reported that after talking about his resentments toward his mother in our group he was able to visit her and clean up his unfinished business in person.

Right after the shooting, his mother was informed by the police about the incident. Smitty was at the station for questioning all afternoon but was not booked for a crime. When he finally did come home to supper, she was so angry that as soon as he walked in the house, she screamed, "Get out of my sight! I don't ever want to see you again!" In spite of the fact that she soon recanted those words, this painful incident was lodged in Smitty's memory. While he was doing the unfinished business exercise with a partner, the memory came back to him. When it was over, he decided that he must go and see his mother in person and tell her of the pain her words had caused him and perhaps listen to her pain as well.

In the group session after the meeting with his mother, Smitty reported how it had gone. He told her he had been going to a group about Getting Real, and he related some of the things he was learning about himself: about how the mind stores false beliefs, how unfinished business clogs up current perceptions, and so forth. He told her about sharing resentments as a clearing practice — a practice for expressing withheld feelings so you can let go of them and move on to forgiveness. And then he told her that he'd been holding on to some major resentments in relation to her and that his intent was to share these so he could get over them. She agreed to just sit and listen and wait for him to finish before she replied. Then it would be her turn to speak. He started right out with the big one: "I resent you for saying 'get out of here, I don't ever want to see you again' on the day Brian died." He repeated it another time, this time in a louder voice. Then he continued with a number of other resentments about other things she had said to him. He was in tears by the time he got in touch with some appreciations, and he shared these too.

When it was her turn to speak, his mother was crying too. She thanked him for the conversation, which she said she found frightening and painful but real. Then she told him something he never would have known if he hadn't shared his resentments: when she was a child, she had been responsible for her little sister losing her right hand in an accident. And her mother, when she was told about it, had said almost the exact same thing to her, "Get out of here. I can't stand the sight of you." Smitty's mom had never revealed these things to anyone, not even to her husband. The opportunity to share this painful memory with her son was a breakthrough in their relationship as well as in her ability to forgive herself for what had happened to her sister. After that conversation, Smitty saw the incidents that happened years ago surrounding Brian's death in a whole new light. Experiences such as this keep reminding me how much healing and transformation is possible if we could just stop hiding and let ourselves be seen.

Taboo Feelings in the Here and Now

Once people accept that they do feel anger and other strong feelings, they can take them more in stride. Sometimes in my workshops I like to give people practice expressing themselves to the other people in the room: "I resent you for what you just said," "I'm sexually attracted to you and you and you," "I long for you to hold me and support my head with your hand," "My self-talk is a judgment about what you just said."

Again, when people do this, they report feeling lighter and freer. One woman, after such a session, exclaimed, "I feel like I'm carrying around less weight!" Another marveled, "This is fun! If I'd known unloading my anger was so freeing, I'd have done it a long time ago." Once people accept these formerly taboo feelings, they take them more lightly and not as personally. They experience "now I feel it...now I express it...now it's over...I'm finished...I can get on with whatever needs my attention next." They learn the joy and relaxation that comes

> Once people accept these formerly taboo feelings, they take them more lightly and not as personally. They experience "now I feel it...now I express it...now it's over...I'm finished...I can get on with whatever needs my attention next."

with being fully self-expressed. They learn to participate in the ever-changing flow of life rather than trying to get their lives to be just right.

Expressing Judgments

Most people hide their judgmental thoughts. In Getting Real, the goal is to be able to take our own and others' judgments less seriously, recognizing that being judgmental, while not always very productive, is an extremely common control pattern. So you're having judgmental thoughts? Join the club!

Admitting that you have a judgment about what someone did or said is an act of self-revelation. You're taking responsibility for the judgment rather than projecting it onto someone else. By seeing it, owning it, and sharing it, you'll get more distance from it and get over it more quickly. Noticing your judgments also helps you to own your projections (the subject of chapter 7). In other words, you *express* the judgment, but you do not *act it out.* Acting out a feeling is when you hit someone over the head with it; expressing a feeling serves the goal of transparency.

> They learn the joy and relaxation that comes with being fully self-expressed.

Furthermore, learning to accept that you have judgments or other self-defeating thought patterns can help you develop compassion for yourself. Often the best way to find compassion is to start by noticing its absence — like when you judge yourself for being judgmental. When you catch yourself judging yourself or others, it's very healing to have a safe place to admit it — in the interest of transparency, not as something you're attached to. Sharing your self-talk and letting your judgments be seen by others helps you get a more objective perspective on that critical inner voice. Then you don't identify with it so strongly: it's simply something you are noticing.

Are there ways by which you inhibit your full self-expression? Do you use obvious addictions like smoking or drinking? Do you have an inner critic that won't quit? Or do you avoid situations in which you might feel too high or too low? Most people were conditioned as children to keep their behavior within fairly narrow limits. Those limits that limit our expression, and therefore our freedom, are what we call our comfort zone. Now we're adults and can handle the consequences of fuller expression, but we have forgotten how to be at home with deep or intense feelings. And we still hold on to the notion that doing so would be too uncomfortable. But I have never found this to be the case. Busting out of your comfort zone might be the most fun thing you ever did — after you get over the idea that you have to be safe, appropriate, perfect, right — or that you have to be anything.

> Admitting that you have judgment about what someone did or said is an act of self-revelation.

The way back to being fully self-expressive is to begin by noticing when we cut ourselves off and then to openly share what we notice. Even if we don't realize until many hours or days later that we have been untrue to ourselves, we can still share our deeper truth when we finally do realize it. Chapter 8, "Revising an Earlier Statement," describes some ways to do this.

Being Transparent in a Nutshell

- Being transparent enables you to express and release emotions without getting stuck in them. For example, sometimes after you report a judgmental thought, it disappears; or after you have been suppressing a deep emotional longing, like a longing to be touched, you may find that with its expression comes a sense of relief or relaxation. You are no longer contracting, no longer holding back. Feeling and expressing things that have been withheld often lead to feeling more relaxed and whole. Your energy is flowing again, and with this renewed energy comes a sense of inner peace.

- Withholding feelings is a way of giving them more significance than they actually deserve. No one feeling is such a big deal — except if you hold on to it and don't allow it to be expressed. When you express a feeling, it usually changes or dissolves.

- Any time you notice yourself lying, pretending, or withholding, you can use this information to help you get back into the flow of life, to get your energy moving again in a direction that you choose.

- Hiding is a treatable condition. It is not terminal. But it does signal that there is an energy block in your system, probably based on some false belief that you took on years ago.

- The way *out* of such a block is *into and through:* feel your feelings; sense your body; and notice your thoughts, fears, and imaginings. Be still and pay attention. Listen. Focus. Don't run away into compulsive activity or addictions. Experience *what is.* Learning to be transparent depends on your ability to notice and experience current reality, both the good news and the bad.

> Busting out of your comfort zone might be the most fun thing you ever did — after you get over the idea that you have to be safe, appropriate, perfect, right — or that you have to be anything.

- Revealing your self-talk as you notice it helps you get over your identification with the ego-mind. It's a good first step toward freeing yourself from taking the mind's shoulds and judgments too seriously.

- When you practice these suggestions with others who have read this book and agreed to support you in Getting Real, you'll find

> The way back to being fully self-expressive is to begin by noticing when we cut ourselves off and then to openly share what we notice.

you have a lot of fun. You'll learn to laugh at your mind's machinations.

IS IT TO RELATE OR TO CONTROL?

Sara heard her teenage daughter, Heather, rummaging around in the kitchen. "She must've just gotten home from school," Sara thought, as she walked into the kitchen to greet her daughter. Then she looked down at the floor and let out a screech: "Aaaaggh! How did all that mud get in here? Didn't I tell you to wipe your feet every time you come in?" Heather, looking sullen, left the room immediately and went upstairs to her room without saying a word.

Was there another way in which Sara might have expressed her displeasure about the mud on her freshly polished floor? Let's consider the intent of Sara's communication with her daughter. Sara's message seems to me to be more about controlling than relating. Her screech and her explanatory questions sound like attempts to make Heather feel bad. Her questions showed us nothing about Sara or her feelings. They were focused entirely on what Heather should have done.

Here's what Sara might have said if her intent had been to relate: Sara makes eye contact with her daughter and says, "Heather, I can feel the heat rising in my face as I think about how I just polished this floor. I'm angry at you for not wiping your feet." Then she pauses and allows her message to sink in. She doesn't lay it on thicker in order to be right or to justify her feelings. Speaking her feelings this way allows her to really feel and affirm them, thus increasing the likelihood of her getting over them. Heather might still look sullen and walk out; she might feel some sympathy for her mom; or she might simply receive the information as feedback. The result of the communication is not what's at issue here. The issue is Sara's intent. When her intent is to relate, or to simply and directly share her experience with her daughter, she is focusing on something within her control rather than trying to control things that are not — like her daughter's behavior. Control-oriented communication tends to backfire on you; it often leads to the exact opposite of the result you were hoping for. It also leads you away from your present experience.

Here's another example of what happens when we control instead of relate. Jody, Freya's supervisor, found herself feeling unsafe in a very familiar way: she had just received a written report from Freya that was full of errors and unsupported assumptions, but Jody was afraid to give Freya any critical feedback. She could just imagine Freya going over

> By placing more value on staying out of trouble than on speaking her mind, Jody keeps herself feeling at the mercy of her environment.

her head and complaining to her supervisor that Jody was insensitive. So instead of giving Freya any feedback, Jody decided to simply rewrite the report herself. Of course, Jody resented Freya for her sloppy report writing, which created unfinished business, resulting in further tension between them.

This type of unfortunate situation is not unusual in the workplace. Jody's need for control in this case is quite understandable. It is possible that she could get in trouble with her boss if Freya did complain. But can you see how little freedom Jody has? By placing more value on staying out of trouble than on speaking her mind, Jody keeps herself feeling at the mercy of her environment. Perhaps if Jody had been aware of the difference between relating and controlling, she would have felt empowered to approach the situation differently.

Self-Assessment Quiz

Here's another quiz. Give yourself a 1 to 5 rating for each item (with 1 being usually not true of you and 5 being mostly true).

1. If another person and I disagree on how something should be done, I'm usually right.
2. I get very uncomfortable when I don't know what's expected of me.
3. I'm almost always in the teacher role as opposed to the learner role.
4. I hate feeling awkward and unsure of myself, and I avoid situations that make me feel this way.
5. If someone gives me negative feedback about something I have done, I'm not likely to tell this person how the feedback affects me.
6. If I'm upset by the behavior of someone close to me, I'm not likely to disclose this.

If you got several 3's, 4's, or 5's on this quiz, your need for control may be higher than your need to relate.

What's the Difference

Relating is motivated by the wish to know and be known, to open yourself to another so they can see and perhaps empathize with your experience. Relating encompasses truth skill #1, experiencing *what is,* and truth skill #2, being transparent. Controlling comes from the need to be comfortable and safe, to avoid feeling awkward, uncomfortable, or unsafe. Controlling uses all the strategies you've learned over a lifetime to make yourself feel safe.

> Controlling comes from the need to be comfortable and safe, to avoid feeling awkward, uncomfortable, or unsafe.

Relating means revealing what is going on with you now, in this moment. By relating as a regular spiritual awareness practice, you will learn to trust that you do not need to control how other people react to you or whether things turn out as planned. Your sense of self-worth will be based not on how things turn out, but on whether you express what you think, know, and feel in each moment.

As you learn to relate more and control less, what you express will be based on your own present-time experience, something no one can argue with, something that only you are an authority on, so you need not be afraid of disagreement. Relating is not about convincing anyone that you are right; it is about shared learning and mutual understanding. You are truly curious about how others respond to you, even if they disagree. All news is good news. You'd rather hear the truth, even if it's disappointing or uncomfortable.

The controlling mind prefers to have things be predictable and known. It prefers that others agree with you or conform to your wishes. It supports having a definite stance or position so that your behavior will appear consistent with your image. And it definitely prefers stability over change. Your controlling mind tries to create a certain impression or to ensure a certain outcome. It likes to make you feel like you already know things that you actually cannot know for sure — like how things should turn out, what's best for another person, or why someone did what they did. As you'll recall, in the story about my dad and his bosses in chapter 1, my dad preferred to think he knew how his bosses would respond, which protected him from taking a risk and actually finding out.

Get Comfortable with Discomfort

Until recently, most people thought of their lives and their identities as basically stable, punctuated every now and then by some big event or crisis that required them to change. Now that we are confronted every day with the fact that we and everything around us are in constant flux, we are being forced to revise our ideas about who we are and what is real. We're beginning to suspect that we are really not in control of very much that goes on around us. And some of us are noticing that we no longer feel as sure as we once did about what we want to happen or what we think should happen.

If our ideas about being in control are illusions, where does this leave us? I think we human beings need to become more comfortable with the discomfort of not knowing, as in: I tell you what I'm feeling without knowing how you will react. We need to learn to tolerate that uncomfortable in-between part of any interaction, that stage of not-knowing-that-which-cannot-yet-be-known (but may become known in the next moment if

> Relating means revealing what is going on with you now, in this moment. By relating as a regular spiritual awareness practice, you will learn to trust that you do not need to control how other people react to you or whether things turn out as planned. Your sense of self-worth will be based not on how things turn out, but on whether you express what you think, know, and feel in each moment.

you can stop trying to control things and stay open). This practice becomes easier once you learn how to ground yourself in the present moment by focusing on what you are experiencing right now. If you learn to do this as a regular practice — paying attention to what you notice — you will experience a profound shift in your identity, in who you think you are. You will shift from seeing yourself as someone who tries to get certain results (and is often frustrated as a result) to someone who is simply aware and present, noticing what's going on.

Getting comfortable with discomfort means not resisting information, feedback, ideas, or events that may be at odds with your expectations and desires. For example, if your mate is hinting around that he or she is unhappy with your sex life, it behooves you to hear the "bad news," honest and uncensored. If you are working long hours and notice that you're tired and grumpy most of the time, you can feel and express your discomfort (relate) or you can override your feelings (control) because you fear that feeling and expressing your feelings might upset someone or force you to recognize the need for a lifestyle change.

One of the best things about feeling discomfort is that it signals, before things get really bad, that something needs to change. If you prefer to be in denial about your pain, you won't heed the early warning signals of an impending crisis (as in "I want a divorce" or "You're fired"). In my study on new human capacities, I found that people with the ability to notice when "something isn't right" and to make the necessary changes before things get even worse are the ones who are thriving in this world of tumultuous change. (See my book *From Chaos to Confidence: Survival Strategies for the New Workplace* [New York: Simon & Schuster, 1995]). They participate with the change process, much like a surfer riding a wave, responding to inner and outer cues moment by moment rather than waiting for a major crisis to call them into action. To thrive in this sped-up world, people now need to become continually responsive rather than occasionally reactive.

Your Comfort or Your Life?

You have probably done your share of controlling — we all have. But where has it gotten you? Do you really trust yourself? How relaxed are you in the face of uncertainty? Are you confident that you can handle whatever life deals you? Is the feedback you get from life really about you? Wouldn't you like to know, before your time on earth is up, how the world responds to your unique ideas, feelings, foibles, and gifts? Or are you content just to give a good performance of the script you were given by society or your family?

Most of us think we would have too much to lose if we were to let go of controlling things and let ourselves be seen as we really are. "There's too much at stake." That's something I hear a lot of people say. To help you take a look at what you think you might lose, here are some typical responses from people I've worked with: "I might lose my marriage." Does your mate require that you lie about who you are so that you can stay married? "I might lose people's respect." Who do you have to pretend to be to feel lovable or respectable? "I might lose money." Is money more valuable to you than honesty?

> When we are fully expressing our one-of-a-kind selves, we also feel more kinship with all the other one-of-a-kind selves in the world.

When I explore objections such as these with my clients, seminar participants, colleagues, and friends, we discover that we're all in this together. We live in a culture that does not support relating. We have been conditioned to measure our worth by how much people like us, how much we get done, or how much power and control we have. At some level of our being, we hate the predicament we're in. We long for the feeling that we are okay just as we are. We long to feel relaxed. We long for the courage to live with integrity. We long to reconnect with our authentic self — that sense of uniqueness and originality that comes from deep inside and is independent of others' expectations.

When we have the courage to show up as we are, we discover that we feel more deeply connected to others. It's paradoxical. When we are fully expressing our one-of-a-kind selves, we also feel more kinship with all the other one-of-a-kind selves in the world. Why? Because when we are fully self-expressed, we become free of unfinished business and are able to be fully present to others. Self-expression leads to feeling open, available, trusting, and relaxed; all things that lead to feeling connected to others.

The Right, Safe, and Certain Game

Most people I meet are still playing the right, safe, and certain (that is, controlling) game. The rules of this game are: project a positive image; don't be too different from the norm; deny or cover up any doubts about yourself or what you are doing; don't rock the boat, especially if this could lead to conflict or disapproval; act like you know, even if you don't; and don't show vulnerability.

Since we all seem to be so caught up in playing this game, how do we create a new social context that supports being real, unique, and open to surprise (that is, relating)? Where did we learn that it's not safe to say what we feel without trying to predict or control the outcome? Most of us came to this conclusion when we were children. We lived in a world controlled by big people on whom we depended for our very lives. We were small and helpless. They were big and powerful. If we offended them too much, they might leave. We'd be without support and nurturance. We'd probably die. That was then.

> Now we are big and self-supporting, not small and dependent. We will not die if someone rejects or abandons us. But much of the time we lose sight of that fact — at least when issues of disapproval, rejection, or emotional abandonment are concerned.

This is now. Now we are big and self-supporting, not small and dependent. We will not die if someone rejects or abandons us. But much of the time we lose sight of that fact — at least when issues of disapproval, rejection, or emotional abandonment are concerned. It does not serve us in any way to see ourselves as dependent on others for our sense of worthiness. I think it's time to stop acting as if we're kids dependent on the adults around us.

It's time to stop acting mortally wounded when someone says he doesn't like something we did. It's time to give one another credit for being able to handle honest feedback. Let's not base our self-esteem on being able to control people and events. As I've stated, this type of control is an illusion, anyway. Let's put more value on seeing *what is* than on being comfortable. Let's get more comfortable with discomfort. We're big now.

If you decide to let go of controlling what others think of you, you'll need other people to participate in this work with you. One person can't do it very well alone. We need one another if we are going to change the rules of the game from right, safe, and certain to real, unique, and open to surprise. A strong movement toward being more authentic already exists in our culture. More and more people are wak-

> Let's put more value on seeing what is than on being comfortable.

ing up to the fact that right, safe, and certain doesn't work like it once did. We're learning that basing our self-esteem on the ability to control external events actually keeps us feeling *out* of control.

In the study I referred to earlier, I found that the people we find most credible and trustworthy are those who are open to our response (which is not in their control). I also found that people who are thriving in this fast-paced, information-overloaded world are those who are able to trust themselves in situations of high ambiguity and uncertainty. This is what an environment of constant change requires of us. It requires that we participate with the process of change rather than trying to manage or control it.

Everyone I know grew up in an environment that favored controlling over relating. Control is still the prevailing cultural paradigm. It is the basis for this culture's dominant institutions: government, business, education, religion, child rearing, marriage . . . even dating! All these institutions are founded on controlling feelings and impulses in the interests of being right, safe, and certain. Control is not bad in itself. It's just that we have become compulsive about it. We operate from the intent to control when we actually don't need to know the outcome or when embracing an element of risk would make us feel more creative, juicy, and alive.

Noticing Your Intent in Dating

Flo and Ron had just met at a singles party sponsored by their condo owners' association. As they were standing in line for drinks and talking, Flo decided to take a risk and tell Ron she was attracted to him. Just then, before she had a chance to say anything, Ron excused himself saying he had to go to the men's room. He added, looking into her eyes, that he was enjoying talking to her and looked forward to continuing the conversation. Flo

> Basing our self-esteem on the ability to control external events actually keeps us feeling *out* of control.

stayed in line and got herself a drink. A few minutes later, she noticed Ron on the other side of the room, talking to a very attractive woman, looking like he was enjoying himself. She debated what to do: should she join them? Should she wait until he's alone and then resume the conversation? Or should she play it safe and just wait and see if he approaches her?

Putting yourself in Flo's position, what would you do? Would you say what's on your mind (relate) or let him make the next move (control)? In controlling, she'd be more strategic; she'd wait to see if he was interested in her before revealing her own interest. In relating, her aim would be to know and be known — to let him know her feelings and see how he responds, without trying to manipulate the outcome and without trying to protect herself from being rejected or to protect him from having to do the rejecting.

Flo decided to take a chance. She joined Ron and the woman in conversation, and when there was a pause, she told Ron that before he had gone off to the men's room, she'd been about to tell him something, which she'd still like to do when the time was right for him to resume their conversation. She stayed in conversation with Ron and the woman, and soon the other woman left to get a drink. Ron told her he was glad she had come over and really wanted to hear what she had to say. She told him of her attraction; he loved hearing it; and they went home together that night.

> This is what an environment of constant change requires of us. It requires that we participate with the process of change rather than trying to manage or control it.

When you let someone know you find him attractive, you don't need to be sure that he is going to respond in kind. If you treat yourself as too fragile to handle unintended outcomes, then you don't develop the resilience that human beings need to cope with a world full of unpredictability and change. On the other hand, if you take a risk, you may learn that you cope rather well with uncertainty. And sometimes, you'll get lucky like Flo did!

Relating in Friendship

Relating is a communication between you and another person that is focused on your experience of the present moment. You notice your feelings and thoughts and the sensations in your body, and you report them simply and directly. Then you see, hear, or notice the person's response. Let's say you're angry at a friend about something she did. We'll call this feeling your "foreground." It is front and center in your awareness, and until it is expressed, your attention will be drawn to it. You'll have unfinished business with your friend.

Relating would go something like this: "I'm angry at you for getting here an hour later than we agreed. I'm imagining maybe you didn't really want to get together tonight." Then you wait for her to respond. As you wait, you notice your bodily sensations and discover that you no longer feel angry. You feel calmer and more available to whatever she has to say. Now, what if your friend gets defensive and tells you, "You shouldn't get upset over such a small thing"? You might notice your body contracting and your jaw tightening as you recognize a resurgence of anger. You could choose to keep on relating: "I resent you for saying that I shouldn't get upset... I imagine I'm 'shoulding' on myself, and I'm noticing that after I told you I was angry, I didn't feel as angry. Maybe I'm over it. Once again, expressing it seemed to clear it."

> After you express it, whatever you were feeling recedes into the background of your awareness. You feel lighter, more open. Your energy is flowing again.

Then you wait, and she says: "Okay. I'll try an I message instead of a you-should message: I resent you for saying you were angry at me, and I appreciate you for telling me you were 'shoulding' on yourself. Hm, yeah, I don't feel the resentment so much now, and the appreciation feels more real."

This example demonstrates how relating allows a natural moment-to-moment change process to unfold: You feel something; you express it. Then you find that your feeling has changed. After you express it, whatever you were feeling recedes into the background of your awareness. You feel lighter, more open. Your energy is flowing again. You got a sense of closure or completion from expressing yourself. And you feel closer to your friend as a result.

Benefits of Relating over Controlling

Relating is like dancing. It is spacious enough to include both partners' experiences and desires. It encourages people to sense their connection to each other, to exchange all the truth, information, or energy available in the moment. It is a vital skill for these fast-changing times, because it increases your capacity for dealing with situations that are paradoxical, ambiguous, or confusing.

Relating helps you develop a very sensitive, even telepathic resonance with your surroundings. This opens up your intuition — a resource that is likely to be very helpful as the information explosion continues to boggle and confound the logical mind. Relating begins from an attitude of not knowing and stays open to perceiving changes and new possibilities as they unfold. Being present and telling the truth are its tools.

In contrast, controlling is an attempt to maintain the illusion that you know how things should be and can make things happen as you want them to. Many spiritual teachers have observed that most people have not resolved enough unfinished business from the past to know what is good for them most of the time. Most people are so caught up in their self-image and in their image of how things should be that they are not able to be objective. They do not know themselves very well — even those who have done years of work on themselves. So when you think you're right or you know how things should be, your "knowing" may be based on a very limited, biased view of reality. It is most likely based on an agenda to stay comfortable, safe, or in control.

> There may be times when honest self-revelation would be truly dangerous to your well-being, but more often than not, most people assume danger where none exists.

When you take the controlling stance, you attempt to give yourself and others the impression that you are on top of the situation. If you feel anything like vulnerability, uncertainty, or anxiety, your controlling mind cautions you not to reveal it. Of course, there may be times when honest self-revelation would be truly dangerous to your well-being, but more often than not, most people assume danger where none exists. When you communicate with the intent to control, you may end up screening out potentially vital information or overriding other people's input if it doesn't support your agenda.

Some Pitfalls of Controlling

Controlling inhibits you from clearing difficult feelings as they occur. This keeps you distracted and unable to perceive your environment accurately. For example, let's imagine you are upset because someone didn't acknowledge your opinion. But because you hold a belief that it is not appropriate to show your emotions, you try to control yourself and push your upset feelings into the background. Perhaps you cover your feelings with a smile, but your smile comes across as inauthentic or forced; and because you did not express your upset, it will still be lurking at the edges of your awareness. This being the case, it may be difficult for you to listen or to stay present to what is going on — because your unfinished business, that is, your unexpressed upset, is distracting you. Your unexpressed feelings end up interfering with your ability to perceive and describe current reality, creating unconscious static in your communications with others.

One example of this unconscious static is when, in an effort to control, we try to manipulate the outcome of a situation or conversation: Teresa tells her husband Terry, "You refuse to hear that I want you to get rid of that dog now! I don't know why we're together if you don't care about my needs." Terry can sense that his wife is more interested in getting what she wants (or proving herself right) than in hearing his authentic response, so he starts to feel less free, honest, and spontaneous around her. He says

> When you communicate with the intent to control, you may end up screening out potentially vital information or overriding other people's input if it doesn't support your agenda.

something to appease her: "Oh, honey, I'm doing the best I can." But in reality, from that point on, he becomes less open around her. He also starts withholding important information from her, such as his irritation about some of the little things she does. As a result, a wall of silence begins to grow between them.

Relating Builds Connection and Trust

Communicating with the intent to relate builds a sense of trust and connection. When I show you how your actions have affected me without implying that you *should* change, then you will feel more connected to me and will be more likely to want to help me. If I reveal to you, "I felt so disappointed that you missed my birthday party," you are more likely to feel empathy with me than if I just tell you what to do, as in "Don't ever promise things you can't deliver!" Hearing a statement like that, you don't get a *feel* for me. There's no presence, no shared vibration. I'm telling you what to do to protect me from experiencing hurt feelings instead of giving you a look inside me.

When I open my heart and mind to you, I am trusting the unknown. In a sense, I am entering the unknown with you and inviting you to meet me there. This leap of faith tends to create a greater sense of connection because I have just risked something on behalf of our relationship.

As you get better at relating, you start to live in an undefended, unprotected state more of the time. You become more open and free from worry. You learn to live without your habitual ways of protecting yourself from the anxiety of the unknown. You accept that you cannot and do not need to control how other people react to you. You learn to prefer hearing an honest response instead of what you're comfortable with. In doing so, you come to trust that you'll be able to handle another's honesty.

Self-trust in facing the unknown is one of the new capacities that we human beings need to develop as we enter an era of accelerating change and increasing uncertainty. Relating gives you practice handling uncertainty and unpredictability. It leads to the confidence that no matter what unexpected events come your way, you will be able to respond creatively.

> Self-trust in facing the unknown is one of the new capacities that we human beings need to develop as we enter an era of accelerating change and increasing uncertainty.

Control, on the contrary, arises from a ground of mistrust — mistrust of yourself and of others. You do not disclose truths that might put you in a vulnerable position until you are fairly sure you know what the other's reaction will be. You don't trust yourself to be able to handle an unwanted surprise: "I'll wait until I'm sure he really likes me before I tell him how much I like him." When you act like you can't handle the unexpected, your ability to do so dwindles. You also lose that zest or spark that comes from taking risks. When you communicate strategically, you are controlling: "If I do this, people will like me or buy what I'm selling" or "If I do this for her, she'll feel obliged to do that for me." Such strategizing reinforces the idea that you have to manipulate other people into liking you or wanting to help you and that you can't trust yourself enough to simply wait and see how others will respond to you on their own.

Control Patterns

I use the term *control patterns* to refer to the variety of unconscious ego-protective strategies people use when they feel unsafe, that is, when they do not have sufficient self-trust to face the unknown naked and undefended. I think most people feel the need for protection a great deal of the time, and most of what we do and say comes not from a sense of freedom but from a conditioned control pattern. I have identified six types of control patterns:

1. *Identifying with your story or script.* Eric Berne, author of *Games People Play,* popularized the notion that significant elements of our childhood stories get played out repeatedly in our adult life because of our scripts. In my family, I was the big sister. This script generated a story line in which I portray myself as competent, knowledgeable, in charge: a mentor and leader. If feelings of fear, dependency, or inadequacy arise, I tend not to notice them. Other people may notice that I seem to be fearful or shaky, but I can sail along through life completely unconscious of these underlying feelings.

Different automatic behavior patterns tend to accompany each childhood script. Take a look at your own life story. Were you the smart one or the pretty one? Were you teacher's pet or a trouble-maker? Did you draw attention to yourself or try to remain invisible?

2. *Filtering your perceptions through strongly held beliefs.* Also based on early life experiences, your core beliefs act as a filter or set of lenses through which you view the world. The most basic question related to core beliefs is Einstein's famous phrase, "Is the Universe friendly?" Applying this question to your early learning experiences, did you feel welcomed by the world when you were born, or did you

> When you act like you can't handle the unexpected, your ability to do so dwindles.

have to struggle right from the start? How supportive was your environment? Your answer to these questions tends to shape what you expect from life and what you get.

Pause now and ask yourself: On a scale from 1 to 10, how friendly do I feel the universe is toward me? Without thinking, just let a number come to you. When I did this exercise, I gave myself an "8." In the story of my personality, I had parents who were very attentive, loving, validating, and supportive — with one exception: if you were sick, they pretty much expected you to ride it out until you got over it. There were no extra benefits for being incapacitated. As an adult, I rarely get sick. If I do get sick, I don't expect sympathy or help. I pretty much expect to take care of myself. So I see the universe as basically friendly, but not very sympathetic toward weakness.

Like my script, my belief that I'm basically on my own colors how I relate to weakness, dependency, and helplessness in myself and others. I may mistakenly assume that someone is doing fine when they are really crying out for help. My core belief structure creates a blind spot. As you look at your story and compare it to mine, what critical incidents or traumatic events occurred that may have given you the idea that "it's not safe to_____" (be sick, be honest, be joyful, express your sexuality, attract attention to yourself, talk back, or assert yourself)? Most core beliefs can be traced back to the need to feel safe.

3. *Getting your buttons pushed.* When you have a knee-jerk negative reaction to something someone else does or says, this indicates that you have a hypersensitive spot on your ego, metaphorically called a button. Buttons are usually related to a repeated insult suffered in childhood. Thus, if your mother or father continually nagged you to do your homework or chores, you may have a button about being told what to do as an adult. Or if they were very critical and found fault with the things you did, you may have a button about being criticized. Using this example, if you do have a hypersensitivity to others' criticizing you, you will tend to hear criticism even when it is not the other's intent.

It is important to know what your buttons are, because they help you take your negative reactions less seriously. Most people's buttons are connected to their "favorite fear," as discussed in chapter 3. The most common favorite fears are the fear of criticism (so you are vigilant for any signs of disapproval or criticism in your environment); the fear of abandonment (so you notice the smallest cues that signal you are about to be left; you may even develop a pattern of abandoning the other first, as soon as you sense that he or she is moving away); the fear of being controlled (so any time anyone tells you to do something, you instinctively resist — even if your mind tries to override this reaction, something in you will drag its heels); the fear of being ignored (so if you don't get the attention you expect, you go into a characteristic reaction, like overtalking, pouting, or some other way of demanding attention without taking responsibility for what you're doing); the fear of rejection (so if another won't give you what you want, you take it personally; you assume his actions are *against* you; it's hard to imagine that they could be simply *for* him).

Your favorite fear promotes an unconscious stance that braces you to survive the feared occurrence. Thus braced, you become hypersensitive to cues that the feared event may be about to happen. This control pattern makes it impossible for you to accurately perceive *what is*.

4. *Gesturing automatically.* Some people have a patterned way of holding their face, their head, or their body. They may have a pasted-on smile or a pasted-on frown, regardless of their inner emotional state or mood. Such gestures are control patterns if they represent your way of trying to remain safe or in control. A perpetual smile,

> Your favorite fear promotes an unconscious stance that braces you to survive the feared occurrence.

for example, may be saying, "please like me" or "please don't hurt me." A robotic nodding gesture might be your way of giving the impression that you are listening, when in reality you are wrapped up in your own thoughts.

5. *Speaking in a patterned way.* If you have a characteristic way of speaking or using your voice, it may be an unconscious way to avoid some feared outcome or to assure some desired result. A rapid, staccato way of speaking, for example, can signal that you are trying

to hurry up and say something before someone interrupts or stops paying attention. Some people who manifest this pattern were not listened to as children. Someone in their early world was impatient or had difficulty paying attention to them. The pacing of your speech and the way you use silences between the words may be your method of making sure that never happens to you again.

You have probably known people who preface their comments with self-deprecating remarks like, "I'm probably being naive, but" or "I don't mean to sound arrogant but . . ." These remarks can be a way of protecting yourself from others' criticism by criticizing yourself first. And there are other ways this pattern manifests. Many years ago I had a colleague who was very demanding of attention and had a hard time sharing the stage. His control pattern was to speak very, very slowly. It was as if he was forcing you to pay attention to him while he took his time getting to his point. Listening to him always brought up the image that my feet were nailed to the floor so I couldn't get away! Oft-repeated phrases can also be control patterns. I know a woman who, whenever she's talking to her husband about something she wants his agreement on, will end her sentences with, "don't you think?" This phrase signals that he'd better agree with her or he's in trouble.

Some people have a constant inner battle going on between the inner voice that wants to do what it wants and the voice that keeps telling them what they "should" be doing.

6. *Replaying the same self-talk over and over.* Your state of mind is revealed by what you say as you talk to yourself. Some people have a constant inner battle going on between the inner voice that wants to do what it wants and the voice that keeps telling them what they "should" be doing. Some continually replay worries about the future. Others focus much of their mental energy on what other people (for example, their significant other) should be doing as a

way of avoiding their own feelings. If you notice a repetitive theme to your self-talk, you are probably caught in a control pattern.

Uncovering True Intent

Sometimes the intent of someone's communication (to relate or to control) is not obvious just from listening to the words. The same words can be spoken with different intentions behind them. Here is an example: "I resent you for saying you won't go to the party with me!" If you hear these words, do you feel the person is controlling or relat-

> People can use I messages and experiential language and still be intent on manipulating you, punishing you, or making you feel bad.

ing? Are you being asked to change so the other person won't feel upset, or are you being given information about this other person with the understanding that you will decide for yourself what your response will be? At times, it is difficult to tell. People can use I messages and experiential language and still be intent on manipulating you, punishing you, or making you feel bad.

If you are in doubt, you may have to ask: "What is your intent in sharing that? Are you trying to get me to do what you want? Are you expressing your upset so you can move beyond it? Do you want me to feel bad? Are you trying to show that you're right? Are you trying to make sure I don't get angry with you? Are you showing me how my behavior affects you so I can decide if I want to change?" Notice how you feel around other people when they are controlling as compared to relating. This practice will help you determine your own intent when you communicate with others. As you become accustomed to making the distinction between controlling and relating, notice how your internal feelings differ depending on your intent. Notice the results you get when you are relating versus controlling.

Noticing Your Intent in a Nutshell

- In most human interactions relating is preferable to controlling because it brings you into the present; it helps you trust yourself; it helps you trust the unknown; and it helps others feel connected to you. Also, most people resist or close up around others' controlling behavior even if they appear to be going along with it.

- Although there are times when controlling is the way to go (when you're on a sailboat in the ocean and a storm comes up, it's perfectly appropriate for the captain to start barking orders to the crew, or when the building is on fire, it would be ridiculous to ask whether people feel like exiting the building), most interpersonal communication does not involve that kind of danger. In most situations, we can't expect others to act on our behalf unless they feel some connection to us. That sense of connection comes from relating.

- Most people exhibit a variety of unconscious control patterns. These patterns limit your freedom of expression. They keep your energy locked into repetitive, compulsive behavior — such as overtalking, explaining, comparing the present to the past, or smiling no matter how you feel. Control patterns reinforce the belief that you need the pattern to feel safe. Noticing and unlocking the conditioned fears and beliefs associated with your control patterns can get your energy flowing again and give you the confidence that no matter what life deals you, you'll be able to handle it.

- In these times of shifting paradigms, there will be moments when you choose to control and moments when you choose to relate. The important thing is to look honestly at what your need to control is designed to protect you from and whether it actually supports your well-being.

5

IT'S HOW WE
LEARN

So far I have emphasized the value of revealing yourself to others without too much attention to how other people react to you. In this chapter, the emphasis will be on being open to the effect you have on the people around you and learning about your effect through welcoming feedback. Welcoming feedback means that you want to hear the truth, even if it's uncomfortable. It means you're genuinely curious and interested in other people's realities. Welcoming feedback is an essential aspect of relating. When you are not open to how your actions are being received, then you're controlling.

Let me tell you a story about my relationship with my father that illustrates what happens when people don't feel that you want their input. When I was about ten, I was always uneasy around my father. He always seemed so busy, so I was afraid to bother him. I had the impression that he just wanted to get on with what he was doing and didn't have any spare attention to give me. So I pretty much kept out of his way.

Behind my family home was an old barnlike structure, which my parents allowed me to use as my playhouse. Originally, it had been designed as a carpentry workshop. There was a workbench and a place for tools, but since my father wasn't a handyman, I got to use it instead as my retreat from the adults. I called it the "Becker Street Playhouse." It was my own little neighborhood theater, where I put on circuses, plays, and magic shows for my three younger brothers and their friends.

One day, as I was planning my next magic show, I got a brilliant idea — or so it seemed at the time. My parents had just given me their old dining room set so that I could upgrade the furnishings in the playhouse. I planned to use the dining table to display my props and the chairs to seat my audience. And then there was this beautiful old sideboard that had been used to store linens and dishes. What would I do with that? As I opened its double doors, I realized that I could fit my entire little body inside. This led to my brilliant idea. I could remove the back and tack a tan-colored drape over the opening so that it still looked solid. Then I would cut a hole in the floor right behind it so I could easily slip out the back and drop down into the basement — a drop of about five feet. As the grand finale of my magic show, I would do a disappearing act! I would say some magic words, climb into the sideboard, close the doors, and deftly disappear, a moment later to reappear at the rear of the room near the basement stairs. I performed this feat of magic many times to the continued amazement of the neighborhood children.

> Welcoming feedback means that you want to hear the truth, even if it's uncomfortable. It means you're genuinely curious and interested in other people's realities.

One day, my father decided to come out to the workshop and have a look around. He still thought of it as his workshop, even though I'd done a lot more carpentry out there than he ever had — like sawing out those floorboards and replacing them with a very thin, easily removable piece of plywood. He looked around my playhouse with a frown. "I don't like how you have the furniture arranged in here," he announced. (I had placed the sideboard in the center of the room to cover the hole in the floor.) "This should be up against a wall," he said as he stepped toward the sideboard.

At that point I had a decision to make: should I warn him or just hope for the best? He didn't seem at all interested in what I was starting to say. Without paying any attention to my protestations, he lifted the sideboard off the hole, stepped on that thin piece of plywood, and disappeared into the basement! Fortunately, he wasn't too badly hurt, just some scrapes and bruises, so later on we all had a good laugh about the incident. However, my dad felt it his duty to board up the hole in the floor, which put a major crimp in my budding career as a magician. I certainly learned a good lesson from that incident, a couple of lessons actually: first, if you let fear get in the way of honest communication, you lose your power to create magic; and second, if people are afraid to tell you the truth, you could wind up in the basement like my father!

> If you let fear get in the way of honest communication, you lose your power to create magic.

The Importance of Being Approachable

Do people feel they can be honest with you? Here is how you can tell: think of two or three significant relationships in your life. Now look back over your interactions with these people in the past year and recall how often these people have given you feedback about how your actions affected them or came across to them or how they would prefer you do something. If you have received feedback, has it been only positive? Some feedback is better than no feedback at all, but if you get only positive feedback, people may have the idea that you don't want to hear information that doesn't jibe with your self-image. (And maybe that's true, so now would be a good time to admit it!)

A postal worker friend of mine likes to tell this story about the importance of staying open to feedback. At a certain city post office, no one liked the day-shift supervisor, Jane. Jane was one of those people who gave the less desirable jobs to anyone who dared to make suggestions about a more effective ways to get the job done. The feedback her employees were giving her was not even personal; it was about how to ensure that all the work got done on time. But Jane couldn't hear it. So her employees decided not to inform her anymore when things weren't proceeding according to plan. "If she wants to think there are no problems around here, we'll let her," they decided.

In the post office, some important jobs have to be done at specific times so that each piece of equipment is available when needed and so that certain bundles of mail are ready when pickup time comes. Unbeknownst to Jane, for more than a week no one was at a particularly critical workstation from 11:00 A.M. to noon, which was just the time these bundles needed to be sorted so they would get out on time. All her employees knew that this station was vacant and that the work wasn't getting done, but no one bothered to inform Jane. It was her job to tell people which job to do, and if she didn't specifically tell someone to be somewhere, they acted as if they didn't know. So they all watched with a certain glee when, a few days later, Jane got in trouble with her boss for overlooking a problem that significantly slowed down postal service operations, not only at this location but also at several others down the line. Jane finally got to see where her "don't tell me

If people aren't approaching you with uncomfortable feedback, you may want to ask yourself how well you are listening. Are you open to and curious about all types of information? Do you ever unwittingly blame the messenger?

how to do my job" manage-
ment style had gotten her.

If people aren't approaching
you with uncomfortable feedback, you may want to ask yourself how well you are listening.
Are you open to and curious

> Curiosity is actually an innate
> characteristic of human beings,
> but if the feedback you received
> as a youngster was overly critical
> or punitive, you may have learned
> that no news is good news.

about all types of information? Do you welcome feedback about
how you are perceived? Are you receptive to bad news? Do you ever
unwittingly blame the messenger? Because Jane's employees
believed they would be punished for giving her honest feedback,
they now chose to withhold potentially helpful information. If you
want to continually grow and learn, and avoid what happened to
both Jane and my father, you need to demonstrate that you are
open to feedback.

I have several friends with teenage children. Whenever one of
these friends tells me a story of how their son or daughter stood up
to them, I always compliment them on being the kind of parent kids
feel they can be honest with. When the people who depend on you
are able to speak their mind to you, it is a testimony to the level of
trust between you. The ability to welcome feedback also requires
that you feel genuine curiosity about how your behavior affects others. Such curiosity is actually an innate characteristic of human
beings, but if the feedback you received as a youngster was overly
critical or punitive, you may have learned that no news is good
news, an example of "learning the wrong thing." You developed a
belief that it's not safe to hear feedback, that it hurts too much.
Practicing the first three truth skills covered so far (experiencing
what is, being transparent, and knowing your intent) can help you
to rekindle your innate curiosity, helping you to shift from seeking
safety to seeking truth.

Self-Assessment Quiz

The following quiz will help you assess your openness to feedback. Give yourself a 1 to 5 rating for each statement (with 1 being usually not true of you and 5 being mostly true).

1. People rarely give me feedback about how my behavior affects them.

2. I do not ask people for feedback about how my behavior affects them.

3. If someone does give me feedback and I'm unclear about what they mean, I wouldn't ask them to be more specific.

4. I do not offer feedback to others.

5. I have never really benefited from feedback.

6. If I get negative feedback, I go into a self-critical, self-doubting mood that can last all day or longer.

7. If I get negative feedback, I usually just think, "That's their problem."

If you answered 3, 4, or 5 to two or more of these items, you need more practice with this truth skill. If you avoid receiving feedback (even if you're doing it unconsciously, as in, "I don't know why...people just never give me any feedback"), you're probably trying to dodge some kind of discomfort — perhaps the discomfort of experiencing a gap between how you see yourself and how someone else sees you. Avoiding discomfort is dangerous and can lead to hearing bad news only after it is too late to do anything about it, like after your marriage is already on the rocks. In fact, avoiding anything is the opposite of openness to *what is*.

> Avoiding discomfort is dangerous and can lead to hearing bad news only after it is too late to do anything about it, like after your marriage is already on the rocks.

Why Seek Feedback?

Feedback between people constitutes a powerful form of contact. The more powerful the contact you invite into your life, the more you'll be able to handle such contact skillfully and with awareness. Asking for and receiving feedback strengthens your capacity to connect and to form intimate relationships. You are letting yourself be affected by another person. Asking for feedback from another establishes the fact that you are interested in her viewpoint and that you are open to learning with and from this person. This practice can also strengthen the trust between you.

> Feedback between people constitutes a powerful form of contact. The more powerful the contact you invite into your life, the more you'll be able to handle such contact skillfully and with awareness.

I often seek constructive criticism from clients and seminar participants. I learn so much from seeing myself through others' eyes. A few hours ago, I got a call from a woman, Enid, who was debating whether to attend my next seminar. She was unsure because she had experienced some discomfort in the previous seminar. I asked her to tell me about it. She told me that in a certain partner exercise we did, she had felt pressure to get closer to her partner than she really wanted to. It was an exercise in which we practiced communicating truthfully about the level of closeness we were comfortable sharing and asserting our wants accordingly. I had encouraged people not to conform to what their partner seemed to want and to stay true to themselves, but Enid hadn't completely been able to. At that point, I realized that I had not given the group enough time at the end of the exercise to discuss their difficulties staying true to themselves. This incident was a good lesson for me. I told her I imagined she was not the only one who had had difficulty saying no or marking their boundaries. She agreed and then said, "Now that I've had a chance to talk with you about this, I do feel like taking your next seminar. I'd like to sign up right now."

> When you allow people to give you feedback about something they have been withholding, it clears the air and the two of you can get back to feeling open and relaxed with each other.

The lesson I learned from this incident is that when you allow people to give you feedback about something they have been withholding, it clears the air and the two of you can get back to feeling open and relaxed with each other. For this reason, whenever I'm coaching people in the corporate sector who want to be politically successful in the company, I always encourage them to ask for feedback frequently from their superiors, peers, and employees. Asking for feedback means that people won't be backstabbing you, because they've gotten a chance to air their grievances and therefore have probably gotten over them. But more important, receiving feedback allows you to continually learn and improve your performance, a vital ingredient in a successful career.

Feedback Practices

There are many ways in which you can welcome feedback. You can (1) ask for it out of the blue; (2) ask for it in response to something another person says; (3) notice something that piques your interest and inquiring about it; or (4) have a regularly scheduled feedback ritual.

1. *Asking for it out of the blue.* If I'm feeling okay about my connection with someone but I want to check in to learn how things are from her point of view, I'll say: "I'm feeling clear about our connection. I can't think of anything I've withheld or any unfinished business. How about you? Is there anything you have to say to me that you haven't said?" Then I'll really pay attention, because sometimes a person will take a while to warm up to the question, and they will

beat around the bush for a while before they discover that they do have some feedback to offer.

2. *Asking for it in response to something another person says.* Sometimes somebody will make an offhand remark that seems to have an aggressive or provocative edge to it. If this occurs, I'll say, "I heard you say, '_____,' and I felt something funny in my gut. I'm wondering if there's something going on between you and me that I'm not aware of." Another situation in which I might pick up on another's comment and seek feedback is if their comment seems confused or unrelated to the present moment. Then I might again state what I heard and ask if there's more going on that I'm not aware of.

3. *Noticing something that piques your interest.* Sometimes another person will act in a way that seems unusual or out of character. Or maybe they've made an agreement and haven't kept it. Then I might say: "I noticed _____, and it seems like something I've never seen you do before (or it seems like it's getting to be a pattern with us, and so on). I'm wondering what's going on. I'd like us to be open and honest with each other, even if it's uncomfortable at times."

4. *Having a regularly scheduled feedback ritual.* If a relationship is ongoing and important, such as with a spouse, a housemate, or a business partner, I think it's a good practice to do a clearing-the-air practice on a regular basis — daily, weekly, monthly, or whatever feels right to both of you (or to all of you, as in family meetings). The next section describes a few of my favorite rituals.

Rituals for Welcoming Feedback

I discussed the resentments and appreciations clearing ritual in chapter 3. That's one good way to keep communication channels open and free of unfinished business. Below are two others. In all these rituals, both people need to agree on the frequency and time limits for the sessions. If you don't wish to have a regular ritual, or even if you do, these practices can also be done spontaneously any time you're aware of needing one. Don't think that just because you have a time set aside to share feedback in two days that you have to wait until then.

Sharing "withholds" is a great way to clear the air. I learned this process from More University in northern California. Partner A starts: "John, there's something I've withheld from you." Partner B says, "Okay, would you like to tell me?" Then Partner A relates something she felt or thought, such as, "I felt disappointed that you didn't get me a birthday present." Partner B says, "Thank you." The "thank you" signals the end of that turn. If Partner B feels a need to bring up the issue again, he can do so during his turn as in, "Jane, there's something I've withheld from you." Partner A says, "Okay," and then Partner B might say, "I feel sorry that I didn't at least make you a card. If I could do it over, I'd plan way ahead and get you something really special." Then Partner A says, "Thank you."

Saying "thank you" is an important part of the practice, because it acknowledges the other person. It does not necessarily mean you are pleased. It keeps the partners from getting into a discussion, since the idea of the sharing withholds ritual is simply to share information about your current reality. Often doing so is all that is needed to clear the issue. Resentments or appreciations could also be expressed within the structure of sharing withholds. So could feedback in the form "when you_____, I felt_____" (described below).

Another great practice is to state, "When you said (or did) that, I felt this." Each person takes a turn completing the sentence, "When you (something specific that was done or said), I felt..." (a feeling or sensation, your actual experience, as in experiencing *what is*). For example, "When you walked out in the middle of my sharing, I felt anger." Another alternative to is to add a statement about where in your body you experienced this: "When you walked out in the middle of my sharing, I felt the heat of anger rising in my face."

All these clearing rituals are designed to be short and sweet. You simply say what you experienced, being very specific, and let the other person respond to the information as she will. You are not asking her to change anything. (We'll get to asking for a change in the next chapter, "Asserting What You Want and Don't Want.") If you find that you need to resolve a conflict or go deeper into understanding each other's viewpoint, then active listening can be useful. In this process, one person is the talker and the other is listener. When it is Partner A's turn, he states his feelings or views. Partner B listens and then says what she heard A say, reflecting back both content and feelings. Active listening is a wonderful tool to use when two people are having a conflict or disagreement. It helps you stay focused on what you are hearing when it might be difficult to hear — like when you don't agree with it. Active listening is most useful in conflict or potential conflict situations, so I'll describe it more fully in chapter 9, "Holding Differences."

Practices for Receiving Feedback

The first thing to do when you have received feedback is to pause and take it in. Notice the sensations and feelings in your body. Notice your thoughts: Do you agree with the feedback or not? Do you feel any internal pressure to conform to the other person's wishes? Remember, it is your choice what you do about the feedback. You are not obligated to change anything. Listen to your self-talk. Did your inner critic get triggered? Did you automatically discount what was said? Did you get defensive?

The first thing to do when you have received feedback is to pause and take it in. Notice the sensations and feelings in your body.

In replying to feedback, keep it simple. After you have taken some time to really take in what the other has told you, acknowledge him for what he has said. If the feedback is surprising or troubling, acknowledge this without agreeing or disagreeing with the content — at least at this point. It's also a good idea to practice active listening if the feedback is hard to hear. This gives you time to assimilate the feedback before responding.

If the feedback is vague or general, or if you're not clear what the other person means, ask her to be more specific. This is important and is different from being defensive. If you're going to learn anything, and if the other person's going to clear the air, both of you need to know what you specifically did and what she felt.

In receiving feedback, see if you can adopt an attitude of openness to learning. Avoid defending yourself, making excuses for what you did, or passing the buck. I have seen so many relationships destroyed when they could have been healed simply because the person receiving feedback could not handle the feelings that were triggered by it and went immediately into a defensive or aggressive control pattern.

It is good practice when you're first learning about feedback to receive it without too much verbal response, breathing slowly and deeply. This helps you learn to fully experience the other's words and your feelings. This practice is especially important if you tend to get defensive or if you get triggered easily. Sometimes quick, impulsive self-expression can be an escape from feeling the discomfort of your true feelings.

When people see you as able to receive feedback and to be with your feelings instead of controlling the situation to make yourself comfortable, they feel heard or received and they tend to trust you more. They also are more open with you about things they might otherwise withhold. If you do choose to verbally respond to the feedback right away (assuming you are not using one of the above feedback rituals that prohibits this), start with your experience as you hear the feedback: What sensations are you aware of in your body? What emotions do you feel? What thoughts, judgments, and self-talk come up? These are what you need to share. "Hearing you say that about me, I feel relieved. I was afraid you were going to say that it's over between us." Or, "Hearing you say this, I feel some defensiveness. In my self-talk I'm debating whether to share this or just take in what you are saying."

Being open to feedback does not mean you swallow the other's impressions of you as the truth. It means letting the feedback in and letting it have an impact on you. Listening to feedback is different from agreeing with it or taking it on. You weigh it against other things you have seen in yourself and in the person delivering the feedback and against other peoples' feedback on the same issue. You are the one who decides whether or not to make any changes based on what you have heard.

Offering Constructive Feedback

For feedback to be useful and constructive, certain conditions need to exist:

1. Both people need to agree that it is a good time to share feedback. You may need to use the preface, "I have some feedback for you. Is this a good time?"

2. Being aware of your intent is another important element. Do you want the other person to see how you are seeing him (with the intent of relating), or do you want the other to change so you won't have to feel uncom-

> Feedback is most helpful and most in line with relating when you do not criticize or ask the other person to change. It is essentially information about you, the giver of the feedback.

fortable (with the intent of controlling)? If you answered yes to the latter, it's okay. Remember, it's *what is*. Don't try to hide it. In fact, "confessing" your intent can serve the goal of transparency and make your feedback easier to hear. Sometimes after you confess your intent and offer your feedback, especially if it is received openly, your intent to change the other fades away. You may find that you feel satisfied just to be heard, even if nothing changes. That's the powerful thing about being openly received: it helps you let go of whatever you were holding.

3. Feedback is most helpful and most in line with relating when you do not criticize or ask the other person to change. It is essentially information about you, the giver of the feedback. Often, by just telling someone how you experienced something he did, you trigger some very useful self-learning. Once I was telling my friend Stan about how another friend I'd hired to do some work for me tried to charge me for services not rendered. I told Stan about my feelings of anger at this person. When I finished my story, Stan said, "When you told me how he tried to charge you extra, I felt sadness in my throat." As soon as Stan said this, I realized that I, too, had felt sadness as well as anger. Stan's simple, nonprescriptive feedback helped me connect more deeply to something I had not been aware of.

4. It's best to share your feedback as close to the time you felt the feelings as possible. But if you weren't present enough to your true reaction at the time, using the "when you did this, I felt that" form works very well.

5. If you notice the other person getting defensive, be prepared to actively listen to him. After hearing his comments, repeat back to him what you heard, including both the content of his statements and his feelings. Doing this gives you a way to stay centered and nonreactive. It gives your mind something to do. Then you can hear him with more spaciousness in your awareness.

Welcoming Feedback in a Nutshell

- Asking for feedback strengthens your capacity to connect and to form intimate relationships.

- It establishes the fact that you are interested in the other person's input, thus helping to build trust.
- Welcoming feedback allows the other person to unload whatever they may be feeling about you and to get over it.
- When receiving feedback, get centered, breathe, and aim to relate — to know and be known.
- When giving feedback, be sure it's a good time for the other person to hear it. Be specific, and tell about you and your feelings. Don't judge, interpret, or prescribe what the other should do.
- In your important relationships, set aside some regular time for feedback or clearing rituals: resentments and appreciations, sharing withholds, or stating, "When you____, I felt____."

ASSERTING WHAT YOU WANT AND DON'T WANT

SUPPORTING YOUR FEELINGS WITH ACTION

"I'm not appreciated around here," Karl thought to himself. "If I resign from this job, then they'll see how much they need me." This type of self-talk is common in Karl's inner world. He doesn't ask for what he wants, because he fears he may be rebuffed. So instead he entertains fantasies of quitting his job. He muses about how the world isn't fair, how people don't look out for one another the way they should.

Carla is in a similar situation in her marriage. She is the breadwinner in the family, but her husband Rudy does most of the spending. He buys himself a new truck. He buys expensive sporting equipment. He buys things he'll never use. But he ridicules her if she spends extra money on groceries to get the best quality meats and vegetables. Carla has tried to speak her mind to Rudy, but since he doesn't honor her wishes, she's pretty much given up. Now she just fantasizes about divorcing him.

Karl and Carla both have trouble expressing what they want and don't want. As a result, their lives are clogged up with unfinished business and fantasies about a world that doesn't exist, about what someone should have done, how people should treat them, and how much better it will be when they are out of this situation. Unless they learn to stand up for themselves and express their wants, regardless of the probable outcome, they can each look forward to a life of "if onlys."

Truth skill #5, asserting what you want and don't want, draws on the first two skills, experiencing *what is* and being transparent. To support your feelings, you need to know what those feelings are. And you need to be willing to reveal that you do have feelings and desires. In my younger days I, too, had trouble asserting what I wanted. I could mention my wants once or twice, but if I got a no or was ignored or criticized for speaking up, after a few attempts I pretty much gave up. Here's how I learned to stay with my wants, even in the face of very strong resistance. I was married to a man who was a graduate student writing his doctoral thesis. He was overwhelmed by the responsibilities he had taken on — being a student while trying to hold down a job and participate fully in the other responsibilities of being married and owning a home. Sex was the farthest thing from his mind. He was in survival mode most of the time. I was in my twenties and in my sexual prime. Whenever I wanted to make love, he had an excuse. Hearing his excuses became painful. So I gave up, stopped asking to make love, and lived in a fantasy world, often imagining my former lover coming to rescue me, showering me with the attention I longed for. During that period, I had a dream one night that woke me up to the fact that I was in pain, more pain than I could admit to in my waking state.

In the dream, I was walking out of a house. I was suddenly overcome by an excruciating pain in my gut. Even though I was dreaming, the pain was so great that it woke me up. And the pain continued for a while after I was awake. I stayed with the pain, feeling its size and shape and location. After a few minutes, the pain seemed to speak to me: "You have to stay with your desires. Do not abandon yourself. Even if he can't give you what you want, don't stop wanting." Walking out of that house in the dream was like walking out on a part of myself.

Fortunately, at that time I was studying and teaching Gestalt therapy at the graduate school where I was an assistant professor. The primary message of Gestalt is "stay with your feelings, experience and express them fully, and don't be inhibited by your fear of others' disapproval." My Gestalt community was a great support for me during this troubled time. I was also working with my own therapist, and I'll never forget something she said to me: "You treat yourself like you can't handle being told no. I think you *can* handle that."

My dream with the awful gut-wrenching pain was telling me the same thing — that I was in pain and that I was able to handle it. Staying with the feeling brought me a deep insight about what I needed to do. I needed to keep expressing my desires, even if my husband couldn't meet them. I had to stop caretaking him, stop protecting him as I had protected my mother from having to deal with my hunger as an infant — by sleeping most of the time. I recognized false belief #2 at work, the belief that you have to shut down your feelings to not make others uncomfortable. I was determined to get free of this limiting conditioned reaction. I recognized that the pain I was feeling was the pain of blocked energy. I decided to get myself back in the flow of life, to stop cutting off my self-expression by pretending everything was okay.

I told my husband what I was going to do. I said that I intended to express my wants whether or not he felt like responding — not as an attempt to control him but to break out of my play-it-safe control pattern. I simply wanted to become freer about expressing myself. Shutting down my feelings wasn't working. I see now that by explaining myself, I was still trying to protect him and myself from the full force of a painful conflict situation, but that's what I did, and at the time, I felt pretty good about myself.

So from that time forward (until our divorce many years later), when I wanted to make love, I would say, "I'd like to make love" or "I feel like making love" or "I'm feeling horny" or "I would love to feel your body close to mine." I said whatever I felt at the time. And I do recall feeling quite a bit of fear just before I opened my mouth to speak, the first dozen or so times I did this. After a while, though, it got easier. I continued to feel sexual; I never shut down and went to sleep as I had as an infant. That was my aim — to not shut down my feelings just because my husband couldn't respond to them. As you might imagine, this was a difficult period of my life. But I was also very alive in so many ways. I was on an exciting journey of discovery, learning about all the ways I tended to cut myself off from my feelings to stay safe and in control. Those years, in my mid-to-late twenties, were when I began to get real.

Self-Assessment Quiz

Are you ready for the quiz? For each item, rate yourself from 1 (mostly not true) to 5 (mostly true).

1. I have trouble saying no.
2. I have trouble asking directly for what I want.
3. I hate to disappoint people.
4. I think people take advantage of my good nature.
5. I empathize with other people's needs and viewpoints more easily than with my own.
6. If my partner wants to make love, talk, or do something else with me, I'm always available.
7. If I've asked for what I want several times and don't get it, I tend to stop asking.

How'd you do? Again, if you came up with lots of 3's, 4's, and 5's, you may need more practice with asserting your wants. Number 7 is especially challenging for most people. As you just read, it was a tough one for me. If your score was high, don't worry — you're in

good company. Many people
who consider themselves honest
have difficulty asserting what
they want and don't want. People
like Karl and Carla are actually

> Continue to express yourself,
> even when it seems you have
> little chance of getting what you
> ask for.

quite effective communicators as long as they don't need to assert
themselves! Both of them, like me, were probably acting under the
influence of false beliefs learned when they were children, beliefs that
were keeping their lives stuck. I hope you are beginning to see how
important it is to continue to express yourself, even when it seems you
have little chance of getting what you ask for. Practicing this truth skill
keeps your energy flowing. It keeps you from getting stuck.

False Beliefs about Asserting Wants

In one workshop a man named Michael was telling us a short
version of his life story as part of an exercise about uncovering false
beliefs. He told us how his father always seemed to agree to do anything his mother wanted — from home improvement projects to
vacations. As far as Michael could tell, his father never asserted his
own desires, but he seemed really happy, unlike his mother, who was
always complaining. Michael's story showed how he developed a
belief that it's better to be compliant and happy than assertive and
unhappy. He had unconsciously linked assertiveness with discon-
tentedness and compliance with happiness and contentment. Now,
as an adult, Michael continues to hold on to this belief. Telling his
life story helped him to see his tendency to deny *what is,* whenever
clearly perceiving reality might lead to self-assertion. Just seeing this
truth helped Michael take a deeper look at his feelings about wanting things. He discovered that although sometimes he was content
with how things were and sometimes he was not, he always acted as
if he was content. He also realized that he sometimes did feel his
wants or his frustrations many days or weeks after the fact.

Just noticing this pattern was a good start for Michael. Even if his reactions were delayed, he was beginning to see that he did have desires and that he did feel anger sometimes when they were frustrated. He started using the tools in this chapter and this got his energy moving again.

False Belief Exercise

If you're like most people, you probably have a painful childhood memory associated with asking for what you want and being disappointed, ignored, or punished. Take a break from reading, and do this exercise: Close your eyes, relax, and let yourself drift to a time when your asking for something resulted in pain, yours or someone else's. When you arrive at the scene, notice who is with you and what else is going on. What do you say, do, and feel, and what happens? Once you feel the feelings, stay with them for as long as you can — until you get an insight, have the urge to speak up for yourself to someone in the scene, or until the feelings change.

When Jane Ellen, a client of mine, did this exercise she remembered something that happened when she was eleven years old. She and her dad were at the mall shopping for school clothes. A new winter coat was not on the list that her mom had sent with them, but Jane Ellen saw one at Macy's that she just had to have. She begged her dad to buy her the expensive coat. He resisted as much as he could, but eventually he gave in, and she got what she wanted. When they got home, her mother was furious with her father and told him to take it back. They had a big fight. He refused to take the coat back, and her mother didn't speak to her father for the rest of the day.

Jane Ellen learned that she could persist and get what she wanted, but that when she did, it would create a big problem. This insight helped her see that her former marriage had been affected by this belief too. She had pestered her boyfriend to marry her. He did. And the marriage was a disaster for both of them. With a history like this, it was amazing that she was still able to ask for what she wanted, but she was. The only trouble was, it always turned out badly. As Jane Ellen went more deeply into the pain surrounding her false belief, she saw that she held the unconscious expectation that if you ask for and get what you want, things don't work out. Seeing this belief, she could then begin to notice the things she did to shoot herself in the foot every time she asked for and got what she wanted. Continuing to notice in this way brought consciousness to a pattern that had been unconscious on Jane Ellen's part. Noticing *what is,* without praise or blame, brings light and energy back into a situation and allows for healing.

> The aim of assertion is not to get better at getting what you want. Rather, the idea here is to speak your truth so that you can see yourself more fully and feel yourself more deeply, allowing you to stay connected to your own flow of energy. Often, when you do this, you also see that getting what you want is not essential to who you are. Experiencing your feelings and expressing yourself are.

These stories show how asserting wants serves the goal of Getting Real. The aim of assertion is not to get better at getting what you want. Rather, the idea here is to speak your truth so that you can see yourself more fully and feel yourself more deeply, allowing you to stay connected to your own flow of energy. Often, when you do this, you also see that getting what you want is not essential to who you are. Experiencing your feelings and expressing yourself are.

Self-Assertion in Dating

Steve had a history of rescuing women in distress. He told me he liked being their "hero" but that he resented how easily they could persuade him to spend money on them. Currently he was dating a woman much younger than he, a very pretty woman named Molly, whose favorite pastime was getting Steve to take her out shopping for new clothes. He obliged because he found her irresistibly attractive and was hoping she'd fall in love with him. He always had a hard time saying no to her.

One day when they were out together at the shopping mall, she saw a dress in a Nordstrom's window that she had to have. Of course, she didn't have any money, so it was up to Steve to purchase it for her. When Steve looked at the price, $450, he knew he had to say no. He was not a rich man. He worked hard for what he had. Molly, on the other hand, didn't have a job; she seemed always able to find men to take care of her. She tried on the dress, against Steve's protests. When she saw how well it fit her, she begged and pleaded, "You have to buy me this. I have to have it. Please, please, please!" Steve rolled his eyes, but he couldn't say no. Fortunately, he didn't say yes either. He said, "I'll think about it," thus buying himself some time.

A few days later, Steve showed up at one of my Getting Real workshops. We were doing some psychodrama to help the participants deal with unfinished business. Steve took a risk and volunteered to have us enact his current dilemma with Molly. He picked the youngest woman in the room to play the role of Molly, another woman to be the sales clerk, and a few of the men to be his supportive alter ego. Steve played himself. His goal was to see if he could stand up for himself in the face of Molly's demands. The woman playing Molly did a great job pressuring him to give her what she wanted. He stammered and stuttered, but he could not get the word *no* to come out of his mouth. After he had tried to assert himself for a while without success, I asked another man, Carlos, to try being Steve for a few minutes. As Steve, Carlos had the same trouble. This helped Steve feel that he wasn't alone and seemed to bolster his confidence. Then I asked Steve to be a coach for Carlos and to tell him exactly what to say to end the conversation with Molly about the dress. Steve whispered in Carlos's ear: "Say to her,

'I'm not buying that dress.' Don't explain. Just say that. No matter what she says, just repeat 'I'm not buying that dress!'"

Carlos did as Steve suggested, as Steve and the others cheered him on. Then it was Steve's turn to step back into the line of fire. This time, he seemed bigger and more confident. When Molly pleaded, he said firmly, "I'm not buying that dress." When she begged, he said, "I'm not buying that dress!" Finally, she gave up. Steve got a big round of applause. And as he walked off stage, he looked each of us in the eye in turn and repeated with a sense of obvious delight, "I'm not buying that dress!" Later in the group we did some work that revealed to Steve his unconscious belief that if he didn't buy people's friendship no one would want to be with him. This core belief was easier to access once he had some sense of personal power. It was as if he didn't need such rigid defenses now that he had more access to his real self.

Steve later reported that he did tell Molly his decision and that soon afterward, he stopped seeing her — at his choosing. He says he values the time he spent with her, because it drove home to him how unassertive he had always been and the price he paid for this pattern in terms of his own aliveness. He told me he'll never forget how alive he felt that day in the group just saying over and over, "I'm not buying that dress!" I won't forget either. He looked so free and so happy.

If you have difficulty saying no, remember that expressing a no in the moment says nothing about how you will feel tomorrow. It says nothing about the kind of person you are. It does not mean you are tight or selfish. It doesn't mean people won't like you. It doesn't mean anything in particular. You give an event meaning according to your beliefs and fears — most of which are conditioned reactions to some distant childhood event. Steve, for example, had acquired the false belief that if he didn't buy people's friendship, no one would want to be with him. He got over that belief once he saw it clearly and started testing it out in reality.

By emphasizing that your feelings and your foreground continually change, especially after honest self-expression, I hope you will find it easier to assert your "don't wants" without feeling it's a big deal. If you're afraid that the other person is going to make a big deal out of it, share that fear along with your no. We'll get into this truth skill more fully in chapter 10, "Sharing Mixed Emotions."

The Curious Child Exercise

In workshops, I often ask people to pair up and practice asserting boundaries with regard to their personal space. Partner A is instructed to take the attitude of an innocent, curious child whose intent it is to discover all she can about Partner B, nonverbally, through vision and touch. Partner B is instructed to notice which of A's explorations feel okay and which feel out of bounds. Partner B then tells Partner A what does not feel okay and what B wants A to do (stop, do it more gently, more firmly, and so on). Then they switch roles. Afterward we all discuss how easy or difficult is was to verbally assert our boundaries.

Try this exercise with someone you know, first as the curious child and then as the object of the child's curiosity. When you are the curious child, what do you want to do but refrain from doing? Do you notice beliefs that certain actions would be too intrusive? What risks do you take? Do you trust the other to assert her boundaries or do you notice yourself caretaking? When you're in the other role and someone is poking around your body or looking at you up close, what do you feel? What beliefs do you notice? What is your self-talk? What judgments about yourself or the other come into your mind? Do you say stop when you feel like it, or do you try to be more accommodating than you really feel?

The two most important skills needed for marking your boundaries are assertiveness and the ability to express anger or resentment. If you have asserted yourself and the other person doesn't seem to hear or respect you, then anger might be an honest response to the situation. Expressing anger communicates that you feel strongly about it. It says you respect yourself enough to stand up for yourself.

Asserting Leads to Intimacy

Anger and resentment, even irrational resentment, are valuable bits of information about your feelings. They help you see yourself, and they help you be seen. They are also ways of making strong contact with another person when the two of you have fallen into the habit of being too "nicey-nice." And remember, you are simply expressing your anger. It is your honest response to the situation. You are not saying the other is wrong or bad.

If you desire intimacy with the people in your life, you need to include all varieties of strong contact in your expressive repertoire, not just the nice, sweet kind. Remember that people tend to be self-absorbed much of the time. Don't waste your energy wishing this were not the case. It's *what is.* Other people sometimes need you to wake them up to the fact that there's another person here with needs that are different from theirs. They may need to hear a strong, clear expression of what's okay and not okay with you. Don't be afraid to get in people's faces when you want their attention. If you hint around, wait for them to notice you, and then resent them when they don't, you are operating from a naive picture of how most human beings are. It's not that others intend you any harm. It's just that most people aren't very good at anticipating your needs.

> If you desire intimacy with the people in your life, you need to include all varieties of strong contact in your expressive repertoire, not just the nice, sweet kind. Remember that people tend to be self-absorbed much of the time. Sometimes [they] need you to wake them up to the fact that there's another person here with needs that are different from theirs.

Asserting yourself can stimulate the other person involved to stretch his boundaries. As I became more assertive with my husband, he actually thanked me for doing so, because sometimes when he tried to give me what I wanted, he'd find that he could give it and that it felt good. He found, for example, that he enjoyed social gatherings much more than he thought he would.

When asserting your desires, you're going to bump up against the other person's boundaries. You might even push some buttons along the way. By bumping against her with your request, you're "calling her out," you're asking her to be more than her limited view of herself. Or you may be giving her practice holding her ground. Either way, it's not going to do her any real harm. And it just might help.

Asserting Lets You Use Your Imagination

One of my main beefs with all the self-assertion language is that it can be so drab. I get bored with all the programmed ways of saying things, even though that's what I'm recommending in many of the practices I teach. So it's a dilemma for me: how to be disciplined in my language so that it supports awareness and responsibility and at the same time how not to sound like a robot. I'm still grappling with this issue. But at least where assertion is concerned, I think I've come up with a partial solution. When you ask for what you want, paint a picture for the other person, giving as much detail as you can about what you want and what vision this serves. When he can see and sense what you're getting at and maybe put himself into the picture, then your assertion has some originality and beauty. Throughout these pages, I have encouraged you to offer specific details of what you actually experienced or are experiencing. Nowhere is this more important than in the area of asserting yourself. Being specific also puts you into the picture, thus deepening your felt sense of your desires. It makes things feel more up close and personal. When you actually see and feel yourself in the picture, you might see that what you think you want isn't exactly what you want, or you may see that you can't accept not getting it.

In some of my couples weekend workshops, I ask participants to write a piece of pulp nonfiction about their ideal sexual encounter with their mate. We do this exercise on Saturday evening. All the participants take some time alone to envision how they really desire to be loved, from foreplay to afterglow. Then they write out their ideal encounter in exquisite detail, as if they were writing a romance novel. Later that evening, back in their rooms, they read what they've written out loud to their partner. The next morning, we hear the reports of what these sharings led to — like acting out each other's fantasies or talking about what's blocking them. Sometimes a few people will read their erotic writings to the entire group. I wish I'd kept one or two of these to share with you. But I'm sure your imagination contains plenty of erotic material of its own!

The Yes-No Exercise

Many people seem to get a lump in their throat any time they need to say no. Or they feel timid about bluntly refusing any request. A bioenergetics exercise comes in handy on such occasions. In this exercise, people pair up. Partner B is instructed to say no and hold her ground no matter how seductive or threatening Partner A becomes. A is instructed to say yes to B in an effort to get B to change her mind from no to yes. And so it goes: A says yes and B says no in response. A uses every tactic he knows, within the limits of the instructions, to try to get a yes out of B. During the exercise, most people begin to project onto the situation some familiar issue from their past or present life. B's nos come to stand for something she has really been trying to stand up against. Person A's yeses come to stand for something he wants and can't seem to get. People become very energized by this simple exercise. The yeses and nos get louder and sound more genuine as the activity progresses.

This exercise shows many people how difficult it is to say no while standing tall, looking in the other's eyes, with their feet firmly on the ground. They discover all kinds of little self-negating mannerisms that undermine their ability to be taken seriously. As I was working with one woman using this exercise, I asked her to listen to her voice as she said no. When she did, she was able to hear her pleading tone. She was saying no in a way that seemed to be saying, "Please, please don't ask me for that. You know I can't say no." She admitted that she was trying to get the other person to change so she wouldn't have to face her fear of disappointing him.

Is Your Assertion Style a Control Pattern?

My friend Mara has a patterned way of asking for what she wants. Whenever she wants my participation in something, she'll say, "You could help me with my x (something she wants), and I'll do y for you (usually something I don't want and have never given her any indication that I want). That's it. Then she assumes it's agreed, and the next time she brings the matter up, she says, "When do you want to come over and help me with x?" I have talked with her about what I notice and feel, and she recognizes what she does as a control pattern. Apparently, this pattern stems from her fear of hearing that someone does not want to give her what she wants and a belief that a direct refusal will hurt too much (like it did when she was a child). So she never asks that question. She's found a way around it. But of course, her way doesn't work too well either for her or for the other person. Whether or not you think you have problems with asserting yourself, pay attention for a while to *how* you ask for what you want. It's a good way to become aware of your self-protective patterns.

A Complaint Is a Want in Disguise

Another patterned way of asking for what you want is to complain, as in, "Why don't we ever sit by the fire and just be quiet together?" When you hear a complaint, how do you feel? And when you speak one, how does that feel? I think most complaints are a cop-out. You're afraid to ask directly, so you complain about never doing something instead of simply asking to do it. Complaints also contain a strained, tense energy, which makes you less likely to get what you want because you're not in harmony with your own energy flow.

Whenever you hear yourself complaining, see if you can discover the desire that's hiding underneath the complaint: "I want to sit by the fire with you and just be silent together." Big difference, huh? Likewise, if someone complains to you, see if you can make the translation, as in, "So, I hear you say 'why don't we ever sit by the fire,' and I'm imagining you want to sit by the fire. Is that so?" As a general rule, use I messages in your assertions. They are a lot easier to listen to than you-should messages. Using these kinds of messages affirms that you are taking responsibility for what you want, whereas you-should or why-don't-we messages shift responsibility onto someone else.

You Don't Have to Answer Every Question

One very common and important situation in which you may feel like saying no is when someone asks you to answer a question about something you don't wish to talk about at that moment. When this happens, give yourself permission to tell him so. Sometimes you won't even realize until you've already answered, that you have been inauthentic. If this happens, one way to deal with it is to "go out and come in again," which we'll discuss further in chapter 8. Tell the other that although you did answer his question, you now realize that you were not being genuine and that if you had it to do over again, you would have told him, "I don't feel like talking about that at this time." If this kind of asserting sounds difficult, rest assured that it gets easier with practice. Remember, if other people

One of the objectives of Getting Real is to stop taking other people's reactions personally.

become upset, you are not to blame. In time, you'll get more comfortable about other people's discomfort with your actions. After all, one of the objectives of Getting Real is to stop taking other people's reactions personally.

Asserting Wants and Don't Wants in a Nutshell

- When asking for what you want, use I messages, not you-should messages.
- Use concrete, specific language.
- Say what you want, not what you don't want. Asserting what you *do* want is a bigger commitment for you, and it's easier for the other to take in.
- Express your wants even if you have little chance of getting what you're asking for. Asserting is like other forms of self-expression — it keeps your energy moving instead of getting stuck in protective patterns. Experiencing your feelings and expressing yourself are essential. The results are less important.
- To become aware of any false beliefs about asserting yourself that you may have acquired in childhood, check to see if you have any painful childhood memories associated with asking for what you want. False beliefs create bottlenecks; your energy gets constricted or stuck. Self-expression helps to free up the blockage.
- Many people have a patterned way of asking for what they want. Notice how you ask for things. Are you avoiding discomfort — yours or another's — with these patterns?
- When saying what you want, practice painting a picture with your words and putting yourself and the other in that picture. Doing this helps you to be specific. Also, your

wants sound more appealing to the other person, and you have the chance to use your very fertile imagination.

TAKING BACK PROJECTIONS

7

DISCOVERING YOUR OTHER SIDE

Matthew was a thirty-six-year-old computer technician working in a large high-tech company. He couldn't stand his boss, Ray, whom he found overcontrolling and disrespectful. His common complaint was: "Why can't Ray just give me an assignment and trust me? I can't stand all his micromanagement!"

Matthew had grown up in an achievement-oriented family, the youngest of three sons. During his early school years, he felt he was constantly being compared to his two very intelligent older brothers by his teachers as well as by his parents. Believing there was no way he could match their accomplishments, he withdrew his energies from school and put them into tinkering with mechanical things. His parents failed to see the value in his tinkering and frequently pressured him to do his homework and his chores. The more they pressured him, the more he procrastinated. Matthew learned that the best way to deal with people in authority was to act like you're listening and then just do whatever you want. Thus began Matthew's pattern of disowning his inner authority and rebelling against outer directives, often unconsciously, by screwing up.

Matthew hated Ray's micromanagment, but he was also

rebelling against his own inner micromanager. After noticing that he always reacted to people telling him what to do and how to do it and that he was always thinking about how these people shouldn't treat him this way, he recognized that the outer struggle with authorities was a mirror of his inner struggle. Noticing his highly charged *should* directed at Ray got him looking at how he himself has an oppressive, overcontrolling inner voice that can't just let him be. "It's like I have my dad's voice inside my own head: 'You should've helped Cindy with the dishes. Did you fill out that job application? Why don't you make a list so you don't keep forgetting things?'" Listening to this inner voice while growing up made Matthew feel smaller and smaller.

The awareness that he was disowning his inner authority and sabotaging his own directives was an important step. This kind of awareness is often the first step in taking back projections that you have put on others — noticing that a pattern has been triggered and realizing that you're really fighting with yourself. I'll take you through the other steps later in this chapter, but first I want to present a more general look at truth skill #6, taking back projections.

> Human beings are like walking, talking projectors. Everywhere we go we see things "out there" that really originate inside us. If you're upset that your mate doesn't listen to you, take a look at yourself: How well do you listen to yourself?

The Outer Struggle Mirrors the Inner

Human beings are like walking, talking projectors. Everywhere we go we see things "out there" that really originate inside us. If you're upset that your mate doesn't listen to you, take a look at yourself: how well do you listen to yourself? If you and your business partner are disagreeing over whether to take a big financial risk or to be more cautious, take a look inside. You may have a long-standing *inner* conflict

around taking risks as opposed
to playing it safe.

> Our inner conflicts are usually
> unconscious. Thus, when we
> project our inner struggles onto
> others, communication can
> become pretty dicey.

Our inner conflicts are usually unconscious. Thus, when
we project our inner struggles
onto others, communication can
become pretty dicey. You think you're talking to another when
you're really talking to yourself! Until Matthew became conscious of
how his relationship with Ray is a replay of a control battle within
himself, for example, their interactions were inauthentic.

'Fessing Up

Sally harbors unconscious anger at men, but she can't accept
these feelings in herself. Instead, she gets judgmental or critical
whenever she hears other women making derogatory comments
about men. She tells her friend, "You shouldn't put men down like
that. Have some compassion!" The first step in owning that projection is for Sally to notice that she has a judgment about how someone else should be. This awareness can be used as the basis for a
hypothesis: maybe if I have a "should" about someone else, it's a signal that I have unresolved feelings about the same issue. The most real
response would be for Sally to express her judgment as a revelation
about herself, not a pronouncement about the other. For example, she
might disclose, "I notice I'm having some judgmental self-talk that
you shouldn't be so critical of men." In this way, she takes responsibility for the fact that she is feeling judgmental. Speaking about it
this way helps her stop identifying with her judgment as the truth
about her friend. I know that when someone has a judgment about
me, it's a lot easier to listen to it and not react to it if she owns it as
her judgment by using the phrase, "I notice I'm having a judgment"
or "I'm having a judgmental thought."

As I've said earlier, being judgmental is a control pattern. It is one of the ego-mind's many automatic ways of dealing with inner conflict, pain, or anxiety. Noticing your control patterns, and coming to know their structure and function, helps you disidentify from them. These patterns do not define who you are, but they can serve as useful signposts pointing how you avoid the truth of who you are.

If we find ourselves projecting, then we can take it as an opportunity to learn. The truth is, we often need others to push our buttons before we can become aware of what our buttons are. Taking this kind of look at ourselves can be very humbling. That's the idea — to become more humble about our righteousness. And noticing our projections helps us do this. So the first step in getting real with your projections (that is, taking responsibility for them as yours) is to communicate whatever you are aware of in the moment, even if you suspect that you may be projecting your unresolved inner conflicts onto the other person. Express a resentment, a judgment, or even an interpretation, if that's what's coming up for you.

Don't try to be totally accurate about what's real. That would be a hopeless task, given the number of unconscious control patterns most of us have. Sometimes you'll need to just say what's in your foreground, keeping in mind that there's a good chance you are projecting. Trust that after you have done this, especially if you do it with awareness of what you experience in your body, you may notice that you are hearing or seeing yourself more clearly. If you really sense what's going on in your body and you really listen to your voice, you are likely to notice

> If you really sense what's going on in your body and you really listen to your voice, you are likely to notice that you have been triggered — which probably means you are not able to be objective about the issue.

that you have been triggered — which probably means you are not able to be objective about the issue. In other words, you are projecting. Once you recognize that you have been projecting, then you can communicate that awareness and perhaps clean up any messes you might have made.

Distinguishing Interpretations from Actual Behavior

We need to clean up our language if we want to Get Real and see things as they are. The mechanism of projection leads us to speak in ways that create confusion between reality and interpretation. An interpretation like, "I see you are feeling insecure" may be a projection. You do not *see* that someone is insecure. You interpret this. The statement is not based on your actual experience of the other person. You may see a certain expression in

> We often need others to push our buttons before we can become aware of what our buttons are. Taking this kind of look at ourselves can be very humbling. That's the idea — to become more humble about our righteousness. And noticing our projections helps us do this.

his eyes, which your mind associates with insecurity. Or you may see him doing something that you tend to do when you are feeling insecure. But you do not see his insecurity. You can express these things in a way that keeps you in your experience. You could say, "I see you looking at the floor as you talk, and I imagine you're feeling insecure." Making the clear distinction between what you see and what you imagine helps you get used to living with the anxiety that you cannot know for sure what the other person feels. It is also a way of using language that fosters owning your projections.

Self-Assessment Quiz

To take stock of your tendency to take on others' projections or to project blame, responsibility, hidden motives, or shoulds onto others, take the following quiz. Give yourself a 1 if the statement is rarely true of you, 2 or 3 if it is sometimes true, and 4 or 5 if it is generally true.

1. When I listen to people, I spend a lot of the time making interpretations about what they really mean or about their unspoken agendas.

2. I often feel that I know what would be good for other people better than they do.

3. When something goes wrong, I want to find out whose fault it is.

4. I think a lot about how others should be or how they should treat me.

5. When I tell someone he has done something that pushed my button, I expect him to stop the behavior.

6. When someone tells me how I should or shouldn't be, I often start beating up on myself.

If you scored several 3's, 4's, and 5's, you probably focus too much on other people, on how they should be and how they view you. Doing so could be a way of avoiding taking responsibility for yourself and the fact that your inner state is your responsibility, not someone else's.

Meeting Yourself in the Mirror

Think of a person whose behavior bothers you in some way. Give the behavior a label, such as angry, controlling, wishy-washy, boring, self-centered, and so forth. Now try on the hypothesis that the other's behavior reflects an aspect of you or your life that you have not come to terms with. Let's say you said that selfish people bug you. This statement most likely signals that you are not comfortable with your own selfish side in some way. Perhaps you are more selfish than you are aware of; or maybe you need to become more affirming of your own needs. Try looking at selfishness as a way of behaving that you either over- or underlearned.

In my case, I have a button that gets pushed by other people's anger toward me. When I was a child, my dad tended to react with anger to what I considered minor frustrations — like the slowness of his employees or minor mistakes my brothers and I would make. I felt powerless to change him, so I developed a control pattern of judging him for his lack of tolerance. Now, as an adult, I notice myself being both attracted to and bothered by men who "pop off" easily. These men serve as my mirror. They have overlearned some-thing that I underlearned, since I avoided expressing irritations as a youngster (heaven forbid I should be anything like my dad!). I need these kinds of people in my life to help me see my own anger, my shadow, the hidden aspect of myself that I can only see by first noticing that I judge it in others.

> So if you said, "If only you would look at me when I'm speaking, I'd feel connected to you," "feeling connected" is an experience that you long to have. Something inside you is getting in the way of your feeling connected.

"If Only" Exercise

Think of someone you are emotionally involved with. Reflect on something you wish this person would do to help you feel better. Use the sentence, "If only you would_____, I'd feel_____. Examples might be, "If only you would tell me you love me, I'd feel safe," "If only you would stop telling me how to do things, I'd feel energized about getting things done," or "If only you would look at me when I talk to you, I'd feel connected to you."

Look at what you have written after the words "I'd feel." Whatever you've written, it indicates that you long to feel this emo-tion but are having difficulty experiencing it. Something internal is blocking you, and you have projected this block onto the other. So if you said, "If only you would look at me when I'm speaking, I'd feel connected to you," "feeling connected" is an experience that you long to have. Something inside you is getting in the way of your feeling connected. Whether or not you feel connected is not the other person's responsibility — it's yours. It may make it easier for you to feel connected when she looks at you, but it is not she who needs to change.

You can use your awareness of this projection to communicate your wants in a way that is real and transparent, a way that takes responsibility for what you want instead of wishing the other person would do just the right thing to help you get it. Own up to the fact that "feeling connected" is hard for you and that you want her help. Asking for help is quite different from holding another responsible. By asking for help, you are actually taking responsibility for the fact that it's hard for you to do something on your own. Here's how you could state it: "I'm having difficulty feeling connected to you. I want your help. If you'd look at me when I'm speaking, that would give me a boost toward getting that feeling of connection that I long for." Owning your projection of responsibility in this way removes the tension or static in the energy flow between you, opening the way for more authentic relating. Another way to take back your projection is to do for her what you are asking her to do for you. Look at her when you speak, instead of worrying about whether she is looking at you. Take responsibility for helping yourself feel connected. In this way, you may also serve as her model.

> Asking for help is quite different from holding another responsible. By asking for help, you are actually taking responsibility for the fact that it's hard for you to do something on your own.

We all project, just like we all try to feel in control and we all lie. I recommend that we all simply cop to this fact and hold our projections more lightly. Don't get attached to them. Use them as a mirror of your relationship with yourself.

How Do You Respond to Projections?

In learning about projections, it is also important to notice when you take another person's projection onto you. Let's say that Jim is angry with you for leaving his car door unlocked and says, "This is a high-crime neighborhood. You should know better than to leave the doors unlocked!" What would your reaction be? Would your body relax or contract? And in your mind, would you start berating yourself for being so stupid? If you go into an "I'm-a-bad-person" soliloquy, then you are not really available to feel your feelings about the incident: you have gone on automatic. Feeling ashamed or bad is a control pattern, a familiar way of dealing with the anxiety caused by not being in control of how another responds to you.

This pattern interferes with your ability to express any sincere sorrow you might have about your actions. It prevents you from telling Jim you resent him for what he said or are judging him for being too much of a worrywart. Anything that prevents you from expressing what you are experiencing will create unfinished business for you. You won't be able to get to completion or forgiveness until you express what you feel or think.

> When you're unable to stay present, I always recommend confessing what's going on for you as soon as you become aware of it. If you're thinking to yourself, "I'm getting defensive — like I did something wrong," share this.

If taking on blame when someone gets angry or disappointed with you is one of your control patterns, notice what happens when you find yourself doing this. Notice that when you are focused on what a bad boy or bad girl you are, you are not present and available to yourself or to the other person. If you find yourself feeling bad about yourself, to get yourself back into the present moment, disclose your negative self-talk. As you may have noticed, when you're unable to stay present, I always recommend confessing what's going on for you as soon as you become aware of it. If you're thinking to yourself, "I'm getting defensive — like I did something wrong," share this. Expressing what's being withheld results in a sense of closure and brings you back to the present. When you are present, you are open and available to *what is.* You're "in the flow."

How to Receive Projections

When someone projects anger on you, don't automatically assume that your behavior is the cause of it. His anger is his. It's about him. The reasons for it are inside him. Even if he blames you for it, this doesn't mean that the blame belongs to you. It just means that he *thinks* you're to blame. On the other hand, don't automatically assume that you have nothing to learn about yourself. Often a projection contains information about both people involved, so take a look inside and see if you are triggered. If you are, it's probably related to one of your inner conflicts as well as the other person's.

When someone blames you for how she feels, certainly this can be a frustrating experience. But remember, your frustration about the situation is *yours,* and you are responsible for it. You may protest, "But she shouldn't blame me! She's not taking responsibility for herself!" You are correct that she's not taking responsibility for herself if she's blaming you for her feeling. But by saying "she shouldn't," you are also "not taking responsibility" for your feelings about the situation. When you assume that you know what another person should or shouldn't do, you are projecting. You have stopped relating and have slipped into an ego-protective control pattern. I'd suggest instead saying something like this: "I feel a knot in my stomach

> Often a projection contains information about both people involved, so take a look inside and see if you are triggered. If you are, it's probably related to one of your inner conflicts as well as the other person's.

hearing you say what you just said. I resent you for saying, 'You made me feel like a failure.' I imagine that *you* make you feel like a failure."

If another person is disappointed with you and you are unhappy about this, you might say, "I'm upset hearing that you are disappointed with me" or "I resent you for saying that you're disappointed with me." Your experience is your own upset or resentment. It is not, "You shouldn't be disappointed with me." It is not, "You have no reason to be disappointed with me." It isn't even, "It's not responsible for you to blame me for your feelings of disappointment." These three statements are about her, not you. They probably arise from your mind's attempt to avoid feeling not in control of how another person views you. If "you shouldn't feel_____toward me" is a familiar inner dialogue, then your control pattern is to avoid feeling pain or vulnerability about how others respond to you by projecting how they should be. What if you just let yourself feel the helplessness, the sense of not being in control? What if you felt these things and expressed them? Can you imagine feeling and expressing, "I feel pain" instead of trying to avoid the pain? Can you imagine not doing anything about your pain, just letting it — and yourself — be?

Another way to deal with other people's projections is to actively listen to them. Sometimes if you don't react but instead simply restate what you heard, the other will get a chance to hear himself and reconsider what he has said to you. Active listening also gives you the chance to see if the shoe fits without accepting or rejecting the projection too quickly. And finally, active listening buys you time and gives your mind something to do instead of reacting. This, in itself, is a good thing.

'Fessing Up, Part Two

If you get defensive when you feel blamed or criticized, once again, sharing your self-talk helps you disidentify with your defensiveness and be more present, as in: "I'm noticing that my self-talk right now is a judgment that you shouldn't be blaming me for your reactions." Your experience is your noticing of your mental chatter. When you report judgmental self-talk as something you notice, you are taking responsibility for it. Doing so can minimize any tendencies you may have to defend it or identify with it.

> Noticing judgmental self-talk can help you stop identifying with being right and start uncovering your own self-judgment.

Noticing judgmental self-talk can help you stop identifying with being right and start uncovering your own self-judgment. You take back the projection by experimenting with substituting "I am" for "You shouldn't"; "I am blaming me" instead of "You shouldn't blame me." You may discover that when another person blames you, you start to feel very self-blaming in reaction. If so, his actions may have helped you take a look at one of your control patterns. Maybe you could even thank him!

Taking Back Projections in Marriage

When you blame another person for your pain, it clouds the truth and makes corrective action less likely. In my last marriage, I typically worked fifty hours a week to support myself and my husband and his (in my judgment) expensive spending habits. At the time, he was in real estate sales and wasn't earning anything but was doing most of the discretionary spending. Thus, it was tempting for me to get into blaming him for my stress level, which I did quite often.

This is known in twelve-step circles as codependency: I focus on how he needs to change instead of on how I am feeling. As long as my attention is on how awful, how unfair, how selfish he is, then I'm effectively distracted from paying attention to me. Yet I am the only one I have any control over. Blaming is great for the ego. I get to feel wronged but righteous. Sure, I still feel pain, but it's pain about the wrong thing. Getting Real means feeling my pain about how I am, not about how the other is or isn't. Pain can be an effective motivator for change, but only if we're honest about its source.

Projecting blame onto my husband for my situation confused the issue. If I really wanted to go into fantasyland and confuse things even more, I could have attributed motives to him, such as, "He envies how easily I make money, so he feels entitled to take from me." (When I am not owning my anger, my mind loves to elevate the self at the other's expense — to prove that he really is a schmuck and I really am a saint.) With some effort, I learned the difference between *my* experience of pain and *his* behavior. I came to the simple awareness that I resented him for buying the big Mercedes and the gold watch and for mortgaging the house. This was my experience. I stopped focusing on what he should or shouldn't be doing. I was feeling tired most of the time. That was my experience. He was not to blame for that. Attending to my own feelings led to some important and very real changes in how I related to my husband. I stopped nagging him about what he should do. I stopped trying to change him (controlling) and continued to focus on simply feeling and expressing what I felt (relating).

> When you blame another person for your pain, it clouds the truth and makes corrective action less likely.

The situation didn't change, so I kept expressing the same feelings day in and day out: "I resent you for buying that tuxedo." "I resent you for not going to work." I stayed in my experience instead of fantasizing about how he should change. (Remember, the goal of authentic self-expression is not to get the other to change.) After about a year of this, I got to the point where I viewed his behavior as his way of coping rather than judging it only in terms of how it frustrated my wants. I let go of trying to make an unworkable partnership work.

As long as I had been focused on what my husband should do, I was feeding an illusion about how I thought things should be. I was not in touch with my own experience. Yet my experience was precisely what I needed to feel and express. I think there's a moral to this story: if you want to make good decisions, pay attention to *what is*. Don't get distracted by your ideas about what should be. Focusing on what should be is a way to avoid making decisions and taking action on what you know to be the truth. I finally realized that decisions about my life need to be made based on my experience, not on a wish or a should about someone else.

> The goal of authentic self-expression is not to get the other to change.

Taking Back Projections in a Nutshell

- Whenever you have an idea about how another person should be, you are revealing as much about you as you are about the other person.
- If you notice that you're repeatedly triggered by something someone does, this may signal that you feel unresolved about this aspect of your own life.
- Understanding projection can help us be more humble about our judgments of others.
- If you're feeling judgmental, use the language, "I notice I'm having a judgment" or "I'm having judgmental thoughts." In this way, you're making a self-disclosure rather than a pronouncement that you're attached to.
- Projections are useful because we often need to get our buttons pushed so we can notice what they are.
- To own a projection, start by communicating whatever you are aware of. It could be a thought, a judgment, a complaint, or an emotion like fear or anger. Then sense

what's going on in your body and listen to your voice. Try on the idea that you may be projecting. If you are saying what the other should do, try looking at it as something you think you should do. While this *should* might still be unconscious, experimenting with your language can help make it conscious.

• When you think someone is projecting onto you, see if the shoe fits you — even though it may fit her better.

REVISING AN EARLIER STATEMENT

8 IT'S OKAY TO GO OUT AND COME IN AGAIN

Cheryl is on a first date with a man she likes a lot. He catches her by surprise when, after about an hour of conversation, he asks her how she feels about him. Instinctively and without really checking in with herself, Cheryl replies, "Oh, I think you're a nice man," when the truth is she is wildly attracted to him. She notices that after she says those words, he seems to shrink down into his chair, as if deflated. She realizes that her words have affected him and that she was not being truthful. So now what does she do? Is it too late? Did she ruin things forever? Maybe not. Picture this: what if she calls him up the next day and tells him the truth rather than trying to maintain an image of being in control. She might say something like, "Sam, I have been thinking about that conversation we had after dinner last night when you asked how I felt about you. Well, I didn't speak the truth. What's true is I'm wildly attracted to you, but at the time I wasn't all there. I think your question took me by surprise, so I just went on automatic and tried to act cool."

Now imagine how Sam might feel upon hearing this. Do you imagine he's going to think less of Cheryl? Do you think he's going to say, "That's it. I don't ever want to see you again"? I doubt it.

> Giving yourself permission to "go out and come in again" is one of the kindest things you can do for yourself.

He'd probably appreciate her honesty.

Maybe you've been in this kind of situation too. Maybe you were stressed or distracted or trying to push your feelings into the background. Afterward you wished that you'd said something different to the other person. Giving yourself permission to "go out and come in again" is one of the kindest things you can do for yourself.

Self-Assessment Quiz

The following quiz will help you assess how much practice you need with this truth skill. For each statement, rate yourself from 1 to 5 (with 1 being mostly not true and 5 mostly true).

1. Once I've taken a position on something, it's difficult to admit that I've changed my mind.
2. I like to get things settled once and for all. If I've decided something, then that's that.
3. I rarely admit to making a mistake after the fact.
4. I find it hard to imagine that expressing a feeling would make it disappear, soften, or change into something else.
5. I would never say, "I didn't really mean that."
6. I frequently realize later what I wish I'd said at the time. But I just let it go, because I'd feel too stupid going back to the person.

Did you score any 3's, 4's, and 5's? If so, you'll find this chapter very useful.

The Monday Morning Quarterback Process

In chapter 3, "Being Transparent," I told the story of Jenny and Fred and their thirtieth wedding anniversary party, when Fred made the comment about the Thirty Years War. Fred had planned to continue by emphasizing how good the marriage had been in spite of the occasional conflicts, but he got interrupted. Jenny misunderstood the remark and felt hurt by it. Jenny did have the presence of mind to speak about her feelings, so they were able to clear things up. But a few days later when they told me about it in my office, I coached them about one more thing — the Monday morning quarterback process. This process allows people to take a look together at what happened. Another name for this process is "if I had it to do over." I suggest using this process after an interaction has gone off course because of one or both partners going into a control pattern instead of being present with their truth.

I invited Fred and Jenny to share "what they wished they'd done or said" if they had had more presence of mind at the time. Fred took his turn first: "Jenny, if I had it to do over, I wouldn't let Harry cut me off. Even though he was trying to

> Any time you see a situation more clearly in hindsight, it's good to use the Monday morning quarterback process. Tell the other person that you'd like to revisit the incident to share with her a new insight.

do a good thing, I could have said, 'Wait Harry, I have quite a bit more to say on this matter.' And then I would have finished my toast to you the way I had planned it, talking about the good times we've had." After making this statement, Fred reported that he felt more relaxed, like he'd taken a load off his mind. Jenny seemed to appreciate hearing it too. At first Jenny had some difficulty seeing what she might have done differently. But then she said, "I wish I'd asked you what you meant by that comment before I jumped to a conclusion. I realize that I often jump to the worst possible interpretation of your words without first checking out what you mean."

Any time you see a situation more clearly in hindsight, it's good to use the Monday morning quarterback process. Tell the other person that you'd like to revisit the incident to share with her a new insight. Then simply say, "I realize now that I wish I'd done (or said)..." or, "If I had it to do over, I would..." Often once you initiate the process, the other person will offer to take a turn too, telling you what they wish they had done differently as well. This kind of conversation can be very healing, both for the relationship and for the individuals involved. Jenny gained an important insight about herself when she did the process with Fred. She saw her tendency to jump to conclusions. Fred also got to see one of his patterns more clearly too — a tendency to "go with the flow" instead of asserting himself. Monday morning quarterbacking can be a very nonthreatening way to invite the other person to take another crack at resolving a situation that may be unfinished between you.

Going Out and Coming In Again Exercise

Think of a situation involving another person that you wish you had handled better. What do you wish you had done, said, or not said? Now imagine going back to this person and telling him how you wish you'd handled it. If you wish, call the person and share what you wish you'd done at the time. And leave space afterward for him to respond.

Nobody's Perfect

One reason people give for not "going out and coming in again" is that much of their energy is tied up in criticizing themselves for not doing it right the first time. If this is true of you, do you really think that you can do everything right the first time? As you get more practice with this truth skill, you will become more humble and more self-forgiving — especially when you see how unskilled everybody else is at the same things you need practice with. Let's lighten up about our human foibles. Almost everyone I know has

> As you get more practice with this truth skill, you will become more humble and more self-forgiving.

had the experience of thinking later what they wished they had done or said or not said or of withholding a feeling until weeks or months after the fact. As you practice this truth skill, you'll find that the gaps between when you had the opportunity to say something and when you actually do say it become smaller and smaller.

As you have probably already realized, Getting Real does not mean being perfectly honest. More often, it's about being *imperfectly* honest, that is feeling and saying what you are aware of in the moment with the understanding that once you've expressed yourself, you'll either see something more or you'll realize your feelings have changed. The impossibility of being perfectly honest is one reason why honest communication is such a powerful vehicle for self-realization. Each time you speak your truth, you get to see it in a new light, which generally leads to reevaluating it, noticing that there's more to it (or less to it) than you thought. That's why revising an earlier statement is such an important truth skill. You're never going to be "perfect, right, and done." You are always in process. Change is the name of the game.

> The impossibility of being perfectly honest is one reason why honest communication is such a powerful vehicle for self-realization. Each time you speak your truth, you get to see it in a new light, which generally leads to reevaluating it, noticing that there's more to it (or less to it) than you thought.

In any situation, all you can do is express the truth you are aware of at the time. So in real life, even when Cheryl (after her date with Sam) does go back to revise her earlier statement, she still may not be ready to admit that she's wildly attracted to him. In that case, she can still tell him that she wasn't all there the other night, was surprised by his question, and would like to revisit the conversation the next time they get together. She could be surprised at what happens next in her awareness, though, because very often,

after disclosing your present foreground, a new, formerly unconscious foreground emerges. And that foreground might very well
be, "And now I'm ready to admit I'm wildly attracted to you."
Getting Real is like peeling away the layers of an onion. Once you
report your present experience, a new and deeper version of the
truth is often revealed.

Usually when people allow themselves to imagine going out and
coming in again, they become energized — a little scared, yes, but also
excited. If you are contemplating trying this process with someone and
you're feeling fearful, tune in to
the bodily sensations you nor-
mally associate with fear, and
then notice whether it's excitement or fear that you are feeling.
Even if it's fear, you can probably
still do it. Remember, in most
cases, fear is simply a sign that you're moving into unknown territory,
not a signal to turn back. Unknown territory is the domain of discovery and the breeding ground for self-trust. If after you can feel and
acknowledge your fear, it becomes less intense, then the risk is probably worth taking.

> Remember, in most cases, fear is simply a sign that you're moving into unknown territory, not a signal to turn back. Unknown territory is the domain of discovery and the breeding ground for self-trust.

Making Amends

If you discover that your actions have harmed another person,
expressing regret or making a Monday morning quarterback decla-
ration may not be sufficient to bring closure to the matter. You may
want to ask, "Is there some way I can make it up to you?" Asking
this question is appropriate only if you sincerely wish to make
amends. And while you're deciding if you sincerely want to, remember that achieving closure is as much for you as it is for the other
person. It will help you feel complete, so you will no longer be distracted by this unfinished business.

When I work with families, I often find that parents do things in a fit of reactivity and realize later that they have really hurt their children. When they recognize the hurt they have caused, they often feel relieved to know there is something they can do. When they ask the child, "Is there anything I can do to make it up to you?" the child is usually very appreciative. Often just hearing that question from a parent helps to heal old wounds as well as the present one. Children are often moved to completely let go of the hurt

> Remember that achieving closure is as much for you as it is for the other person. It will help you feel complete, and you will not be distracted by this unfinished business.

they were carrying: "No, I don't need anything from you. Just hearing that you're sorry means a lot." I coach children not to be too easy on their parents, however, especially if the child has a pattern of protecting the parent from discomfort. The act of deciding on something a parent can do for you and then asking for it can create an even more profound healing — for the parent as well as the child.

Sometimes children do dumb things that cause real harm to their parents also. I recall one meeting I had with a father and son. Timmy had broken his dad's expensive wristwatch, and Leon, Timmy's dad, was expressing his anger. When Timmy asked, "Is there anything I can do to make it up to you?" Leon got a big grin on his face, gave his son a hug, and said, "Let's make a list." Working together they came up with a list of ten things that Timmy would do to help him and his dad get closure on the incident — things like "wash my truck every month for the next year," "cook me breakfast," and "do your homework without being nagged." What started out as an extremely traumatic family therapy session for Timmy ended up being empowering and fun. It also gave both father and son some practice at win-win negotiating.

Making Amends Exercise

Think of a situation in which you did something that harmed another person. Recall exactly what you did or said, being as specific as possible. Notice any tendency you may have to lay a guilt trip on yourself. Guilt tripping can be a kind of control pattern, a patterned way of dealing with mistakes or transgressions. It can lead you to focus more on how wrong you were (a judgment) than on what you actually did and how you feel (your experience).

If you find yourself feeling guilty, come back to the specifics of what you did and how you feel about what you did and about the consequences. Notice how you actually feel. Doing this instead of focusing on what a bad person you are is much more constructive. Now make a list of things you might do for the person to make it up to them, to make amends. If you wish, call her and arrange a time to meet in person so you can actually express to her what you feel and what you are willing to do about it. Let the other person have a voice in the decision about what you do to make your amends.

Admitting a Lie

You can also practice revising an earlier statement when you have lied and want to come clean about it. We all hate to get caught in a lie. But it happens. It has happened more than once to people in high office, such as the U.S. presidency. In my experiences with people in less lofty places — in marriages and in work teams — I have been amazed to see how forgiving people are when someone admits to having lied.

In a mid-sized manufacturing company where I consulted, a certain manager, Sal, tried to cover up the fact that his actions had been responsible for hundreds of thousands of dollars of damage to a piece of company equipment. I could see that everyone knew that Sal was responsible. But Sal maintained his position that an outside vendor had been to blame for the accident. While the incident was under investigation, the company president, Tom, came to me and confided, "If Sal tries to deny his responsibility for this, he's history. I don't want him in my company. But if he'll come out and admit his mistake, I'll gladly forgive him. Everyone makes mistakes. Lying and maintaining your innocence sets a bad example. I can't tolerate that around here." I thought to myself, "If only Sal could hear this." So I shared this thought with Tom and then asked, "Is there any way you'd be willing to say this publicly?" Tom affirmed that it was not his job to give Sal an easy way out; if Sal was a person of integrity, he'd come clean. If not, so be it.

After that conversation with Tom, I wrestled with how to get more authentic communication happening between these two men about the incident. Finally, I realized that I had to be authentic about my own feelings. I couldn't take responsibility for others' authenticity. So I set up a time to tell Tom "what I wish I'd said," which was: "Tom, now I know a secret of yours that you don't want me to divulge. I'm angry with you for telling me something without first letting me know that you were entrusting me with a secret. I would have said that I can't guarantee that I'll keep it. I don't feel good about keeping secrets, especially when I think what you said about admitting mistakes is something everyone in your company would want to know. It's vital information about the culture you are envisioning around here."

This disclosure moved Tom to make a public general statement about his vision of a company that tolerated and forgave mistakes if they were owned up to and if amends were made. When Sal heard this, he was still reluctant. He had been punished often in the past for telling the truth about his mistakes. But after some deliberation, he did go to Tom personally. He described the entire incident — what he did, how he felt afterward, how he felt about lying, his fears about telling the truth, and how he alone was responsible for the damage. He was amazed to find that Tom received his disclosure with compassion and an attitude of forgiveness. At my suggestion, Tom later went back to Sal to share more of what he'd felt before Sal's confession — the anger, the judgment, the fear of losing Sal as a worker. Once that conversation occurred, both men felt complete, and everyone could put the incident behind them and get back to work.

Steps To Take When Revising

Practicing this truth skill helps you let go of feelings you are carrying, thus bringing you more into the present. It also gives the other person a chance to get over whatever he may have been carrying about you. It's a good way to bring your relationship up to date, to clear the air. There are several steps you can take when dealing with any situation that needs revising. They are:

1. First let the other person know that you have had some second thoughts and make sure you have their attention; invite them into conversation by stating that you'd like to revise what you said or did.

2. Don't make excuses. Take responsibility for your words or deeds.

3. Then report what has changed for you — what you are aware of now that you were not aware of at the time: "I had the realization that..." "I want to let you know what was really going on with me..." "I want to make amends...," and so on. In this step, use all the communication tools we have already identified in this book. Use I messages to help you stay in your own experience.

4. And finally listen to what the other person has to say, and aim to be more present this time. Leave space for the other to take a turn saying how she wishes she'd done things differently also, if she seems so inclined.

If you give yourself permission to revise and revisit whenever you need to, then you'll take each interaction more lightly. You don't have

to try so hard to get things perfect the first time. Most things
we do are not cast in stone. Yes,
your words may have hurt
someone. Or yes, you may have
been too agreeable and now you
are disappointing someone.

> If you give yourself permission to revise and revisit whenever you need to, then you'll take each interaction more lightly. You don't have to try so hard to get things perfect the first time.

When your revision comes from an authentic place, usually the other
person will sense the caring that it takes to make the effort to go out
and come in again. And even if he doesn't, you'll live.

Revising in a Nutshell

- Often when you learn how your actions have affected
  another person, you feel sincere regret or empathy or you
  see more of the whole picture and realize that you were
  reacting from a pattern.
- Sharing your afterthoughts is a way of clearing things up.
- When you realize your actions have harmed another person, offering to make amends is another way of clearing
  things up.
- Sometimes after you state what you wish you'd done or said
  differently, the other person joins you and makes a revision
  of her own.
- When these tools for revising an earlier statement are used
  by people in a conflict situation, they usually foster a softer,
  more openhearted attitude between conflicting parties.
- After you use this truth skill for a while, you will probably
  notice that the gap between when you could have said
  something and when you actually do gets smaller. By going
  out and coming in again, you train yourself to be more
  present the next time.

HOLDING DIFFERENCES

9

SEEING OTHER VIEWPOINTS
WITHOUT LOSING YOUR OWN

In the martial art of aikido, being centered means the ability to engage and face the world as your "opponent" faces the world, seeing from the other's viewpoint without losing your own. And so it is in life: if you want to see reality clearly and take action based on all available input, you must be able to hold differences — to maintain your own viewpoint while considering other people's views. This truth skills enables you to take in several perspectives at once so you can consider them in relation to one another. It allows you to see more of what is actually going on rather than narrowing your vision to feel right, safe, or certain. Your consciousness becomes spacious and nonreactive, and you can see your options more clearly.

In dealing with differences or disagreements, you basically have three choices: you can try to get other people to see things your way; you can give in to others to minimize conflict; or you can practice holding differences — truth skill #8. Many people assume they have only the first two choices — to dominate or to submit. But in a world full of complexity and change, these first two options lead to solutions that are often simplistic or shortsighted. Holding differences enables you to draw a bigger circle around two or more competing views so that you can see how they are complementary parts of a whole instead of mutually exclusive.

A famous Sufi teaching story relates how three blind men encountered an elephant as they were walking down the road one day. The first blind man came upon the elephant's side and asserted to his companions, "The road ends here. We have come to a wall." The second bumped into one of the elephant's legs, wrapped his arms around it, and protested, "No, it is only a tree." A moment later the third blind man came into contact with the elephant's tail and assured his cohorts, "It most certainly is nothing but a rope." This story challenges belief systems based on dualistic, either-or interpretations of reality. Humanity as a whole is very much like those three blind men, each clinging to a little piece of the truth and ignoring how that piece might fit with others in an attempt to remain right, safe, and certain. At some point in our histories, we learned to fear differences. We got the idea that if you see one thing, and I see something else, one of us must be wrong; or if you want one thing and I want something else, one of us must lose. We learned that if a person reveals his unique point, angle, or range of view, he is opening himself up to being challenged.

> In dealing with differences or disagreements, you basically have three choices: you can try to get other people to see things your way; you can give in to others to minimize conflict; or you can practice holding differences.

To find harmony in this world of diversity, we need to embrace paradox. We need to recognize both the inevitability of disagreement between people and the possibility of harmony through approaching conflict as an opportunity to see more of what is really going on. It takes more than one blind man to "see" the whole elephant!

Self-Assessment Quiz

The following quiz will help you to assess how skillful you are at holding differences. For each statement, rate yourself from 1 to 5 (with 1 being usually not true and 5 being usually true).

1. I avoid people who have values and beliefs very different from mine.
2. When someone is angry or disappointed with me, it's hard for me to simply let him feel what he feels. I try to explain my side of things so he won't feel angry anymore.
3. It's easy for me to lose myself in an intimate relationship.
4. I tend to be swayed by strong arguments delivered with confidence.
5. After listening to someone who strongly and forcefully disagrees with me, I sometimes forget what I was about to say.
6. I think when two people strongly disagree, one of them will have to give in eventually if they want to preserve the relationship.
7. I avoid getting too interdependent with anyone — like in a committed relationship or a business partnership.
8. I get upset when someone I respect disagrees with me.

How skilled are you at holding your own viewpoint in the face of strong opposition? Do you welcome or avoid situations that force you to confront differences? If you scored mostly 3's, 4's, and 5's, you probably need more practice with this truth skill.

> It takes more than one blind man to "see" the whole elephant!

In my experience as a consultant and coach to business leaders and entrepreneurs, I have found that it is not just the timid who have trouble holding differences. As the head of a multibillion-dollar company once said to me: "Why do you think I started my own company? So I can tell people what to do! So I can get my own way all the time!" I know this comment was offered somewhat tongue in cheek, but I think it's partially true for many leaders. They get into positions of power so they can avoid dealing with conflict. Of course, what you avoid in life has a way of coming back to bite you in the backside. That's what these executives eventually discover. The more you try to avoid conflict the more havoc it plays with your well-laid plans.

At some point we learn to accept diversity as a fact of life. While human beings do have similar basic needs, we each view the world from our own unique angle or perspective. This uniqueness is our contribution to the human story. It's what we have to teach one another.

We're All Conflict Challenged

Most people have learned to mask the ways in which they differ from the social norm. When you were a child and dependent on adults for your survival, you may have learned that it's not safe to be too different. Maybe the grown-ups ridiculed you or tried to get you to conform. So you decided that it was best to keep your most original and unique views to yourself. As children most of us learned that the big people are usually right, and the little people are usually wrong. So if you still unconsciously see yourself as little, your behavior may be governed by the false belief that if you express your view and it's different from someone else's, his view will win, so it's best just to avoid the whole situation. Instead of holding the difference between your two perspectives, you just conform or pretend to agree. It's safer that way.

Getting Real is a cooperative project. We're all conflict challenged to some degree. Each person who admits it and goes about learning to hold differences without making either party wrong contributes to healing our collective wound. The only way the world

> The only way the world will ever be a safe place to express our full uniqueness is if we can learn together that your view need not pose a threat to mine.

will ever be a safe place to express our full uniqueness is if we can learn together that your view need not pose a threat to mine.

From Despair to Unity

I'd like to tell you about an experience I had a few weeks ago at a ten-day silent Vipassana meditation retreat. The experience showed me not only that your view need not pose a threat to mine but also that all views are part of one unified whole when seen with enough perspective. It also reminded me that when you go completely and with awareness into whatever pain you might be feeling, it can lead you to another level of consciousness.

On the eighth day of the retreat, after we had been sitting in meditation for an hour, my teacher suggested that some of us might want to do a standing meditation for the next hour of the scheduled "sit." I chose to take the standing posture at that point. After standing for about ten minutes, I began to sense what I can only call an ancient memory of myself as a primitive, aboriginal being. I was simply standing there, in a state of wonder and innocence, all the while repeating the mantra that my teacher had given me to work with on that occasion. Then I heard the sounds of an airplane flying over our retreat center. As I stood there, so open and sensitive, it seemed as if I could smell some of the air pollution that was raining down on earth from the plane's exhaust.

Listening to these sounds, breathing consciously, and repeating my mantra, I began to experience a sharp pain around my heart. As I focused on it, the pain radiated outward to my entire torso. I felt like doubling over, but I did not. I just stood there. The pain continued as I listened to the airplane overhead. Finally, I could contain it no longer, and I burst into deeply felt sobs — sobbing for the pain of the earth and its people, for the ways we are polluting our own sources of food and water and air. The sounds of my sobbing filled the meditation hall, as the other meditators continued quietly with their practice. Then I heard another plane overhead, and the pain became even more intense. I cried out in my pain. It was almost more than my body could bear. I felt what could only be described in human terms as despair — complete hopelessness and helplessness. There was nothing I could do and nothing to be done to change *what is*. All I could do was feel and express what I felt. And all the while I was standing in that warrior-like posture, feet firmly on the ground, knees slightly bent, spine erect.

After about twenty or thirty minutes of deep sobbing, I heard a third plane fly over us. This time, as I let the engine's sounds enter me, still sensing the pollution raining down on all of us, I felt as if I were on that plane. I could be on a business trip, wearing a suit, sitting there working on my laptop computer. I was the polluter as well as the one being polluted. My crying eased as I listened further to the sounds of the world outside, the music of the spheres. I heard a bird chirping. And I sensed a oneness with that bird. I heard dogs barking, and I became those dogs. Another plane flew over, and I felt myself expand to embrace all these creatures, natural and unnatural, animate and inanimate. As I stood in the hall, still repeating my mantra and breathing consciously, my emotions grew calmer. Yet my physical self was vibrating at a level that I had never experienced before. I was buzzing, tingling, humming at a very refined, yet intense, level. This experience was beyond words, as all real experiences are. I felt so expanded. I felt whole. When the gong sounded

> I was the polluter as well as the one being polluted.

signaling that the "sit" was over, I lay down on the floor to rest. As I lay there my body was vibrating in such a way that I actually felt myself levitating off the floor slightly. I imagine that if someone could have weighed my body at that point, I would have weighed less than my usual weight.

In this experience I embraced paradox as an aspect of human existence. Within myself I held the difference, or contained the ten-

> When you hold differences between two seemingly opposite poles or positions, your consciousness actually expands, and you become a "bigger" person.

sion, between the polluters and those suffering from the pollution. There was no one *out there* at whom to point the finger of blame. I can still recall vividly the pain in my heart, in my emotional body. But afterward there was also an expansiveness to the sensation. It became a tension I expanded with instead of contracting into. I experienced how, when you hold differences between two seemingly opposite poles or positions, your consciousness actually expands, and you become a "bigger" person.

Contact-Withdrawal Exercise

In my Getting Real workshops, many of the learning activities focus on becoming aware of people's differing contact-withdrawal rhythms — the fact that in any relationship, at any given moment, one person may feel like withdrawing when the other feels like being in contact. Here is an exercise you can try with a partner.

Sit facing your partner. Close your eyes and focus your attention inward for a while. Then, when you are ready, focus your attention outward on your partner and make nonverbal contact in whatever form feels authentic. Remember that the level and pacing of contact that feels good to one person is usually different from what feels right to the other. Any two people are likely to have different rhythms regarding when they feel like being in contact and when they feel like focusing their attention inward.

Continue to face each other, paying attention to when you feel like being in contact and when you feel like withdrawing your focus inward. Make it your goal to be as true as possible to your own rhythms — staying in contact or available when you feel like it regardless of what the other person is doing and withdrawing into yourself whenever you feel like it, even if the other appears to want contact. Remain face-to-face, with eyes open or closed depending on your feeling at the moment, and follow your own flow of contact and withdrawal. After the exercise, when people share their thoughts, feelings, and observations about the exercise, many notice how much easier it is to "be themselves" with their eyes closed. They also mention how challenging it is to withdraw from their partner when the partner seems to want contact and how hard it is to stay in contact when the other is pulling away. The human ego has a tendency to see differing wants as a problem, rather than as simply *what is.* People attach way too much meaning to the simple phenomenon of differing rhythms. The purpose of the contact-withdrawal exercise is to demonstrate that people can allow themselves to experience a difference in contact rhythms without any threat to their present well-being.

Active Listening

Everyone knows how important it is to listen — to take in what another person is saying and to let her know she is being heard. Holding differences is a kind of advanced listening. To practice this truth skill, you need to be able to listen to things you'd rather not hear, things that challenge your point of view, or even things that push your buttons.

Holding differences depends on your ability to assert your boundaries. You know what you feel and want and value, and you don't let anybody mess with those things unless you so choose. This allows you to both have your own experience and to be open to alternative views. You can consider more information all at once without getting confused. You can actually hold several perspectives in your mind and consider them simultaneously and in relation to one another. Doing this deepens your intuitive decision making and creative problem solving, because it catapults you out of the limitations of dualistic, black-and-white thinking.

I mentioned active listening in chapter 5 when I talked about how to keep yourself from overreacting to feedback. When you practice active listening, you discipline yourself to pay attention by repeating back to the speaker what he has just said. This is the best tool I know for developing the ability to hold differences. I offer an example of how this works in the following interaction.

Holding Differences at Work

Jake is asking his supervisor, Mory, for a raise. Mory learned about active listening in a communications seminar he took last year. Jake, on the other hand, has never heard of active listening. When Mory learns Jake's agenda, he knows he had better start out listening actively so that he won't react too quickly and so that he'll really be able to listen to what Jake has to say.

Jake: I've been working for you for four years, and I'm still making $25 an hour. I think I'm the best mechanic on the fleet. And I know for a fact some of the other guys make the same as me.

Mory: You're thinking you've been here four years and are still working for $25 an hour and that others, who aren't as valuable to the company as you, are getting the same pay. Did I hear you right?

Jake: Yeah. I think I'm worth more money.

Mory: You think you deserve more money. And you're hoping I think so too — is that right? Okay, now can I tell you how I see it?

Jake: Sure.

Mory: I see your point of view, and I appreciate you for coming to talk to me. I'm sympathetic to what you said. I think you are worth more than you're getting. At the same time, I'm seeing a different part of the picture. I'd like to tell you what's up for me these days.

Jake: Yeah, go ahead.

Mory: As the general manager, I'm feeling a lot of pressure from the competition. I'm afraid if I spend any more on salaries, the company won't be able to put the amount of money we need into new advertising that we need to do to stay competitive. I know you're worth more than you're getting. I just haven't figured out how to give you what you deserve and still have my budget work over the long haul.

Jake: Is there anything I can do to help with what you're talking about?

Mory: You're thinking maybe you can help? Well, I don't know. Let me think about that.

Mory goes away and reflects on the conversation. He lets both Jake's words and his own rattle around in his brain for a while. He remembers Jake's question, "Is there anything I can do to help?" That night he has an idea just as he is falling off to sleep: he envisions all the mechanics helping to bring in customers. He develops a plan for how they can help the company stay competitive in a way that is unusual but not unrealistic. The next day he tries this idea out on Jake, asking if he would be willing to participate in a word-of-mouth advertising campaign. Jake likes the idea. They spend some time fleshing out a plan to bring to the other mechanics. In the end, Mory is able to cut down on his advertising budget due to the expanded public-relations role of his employees. They all decide that those who participate most effectively in the new plan will earn either raises or bonuses as a result of their increased efforts. This would enable Jake to get the raise he was seeking.

This example shows how when two people with opposing interests listen to each other, a win-win solution can often be found. Mory used active listening to hold the difference between his view and Jake's. He really listened to Jake, even when doing so was uncomfortable. At the same time he held true to his own point of view. After considering both views, he found that something Jake said had given him an idea for how both people's needs might be met.

> Active listening builds mutual understanding and often provides the information needed for discovering mutually beneficial solutions. The goodwill created generates creative energy — in contrast to the mistrust and with-holding of information that occurs in most situations where there is a conflict of interests.

Active listening builds mutual understanding and often provides the information needed for discovering mutually beneficial solutions. The goodwill created generates creative energy — in contrast to the mistrust and withholding of information that occurs in most situations where there is a conflict of interests.

Holding Differences in Marriage

Paula is fifty. Paul is forty-six. They have been married for ten years. This is the second marriage for both. When they first got together, they agreed to be monogamous, but now things have changed. Paul believes he has "only a few good years left" in terms of his sexual vitality. He has only had four sexual partners in his life, and he's feeling a need to experiment with other lovers. He also has the idea that being monogamous is killing his passion and his sense of vitality as a man. He sincerely believes that it is dishonest for him to pretend to be satisfied with just one sex partner. He loves Paula and enjoys what he and she have together, but he keeps noticing his sexual attention being drawn toward other women.

Paula is beside herself with grief and anger. She wants to stay monogamous. She believes that sex is a sacred act, and she has not had any desire to be with other sex partners. They have arrived at a true impasse. Paul feels strongly that he cannot be true to himself and stay monogamous. He also feels genuine empathy for Paula. It hurts him to see her in pain. Paula imagines that if Paul has sex with other women, she will not be able to be as open and vulnerable with him. She trusts what Paul says about himself — that he feels dishonest pretending to be monogamous. She wants Paul to have what he wants, and at the same time, she thinks she'd be untrue to herself staying in a nonmonogamous relationship. Paul wants Paula to feel safe and open with him.

> If you can stay in the impasse for enough time, allowing the difference to exist rather than rushing prematurely to a resolution, you will be changed by the experience. This change is not predictable. It doesn't take the form of giving in or compromising but rather of expanding yourself.

If you were Paul or Paula, can you imagine how you might experience such a predicament? Can you imagine feeling two contradictory things at once: the wish to have what you want alongside the wish for your partner to have what he or she wants? This is what it feels like to hold differences. It's like hanging out in an unresolved predicament without knowing if there will be a resolution. Some people can't stand the tension, so they jump to a premature conclusion — like "I'm out of here" or "I know I'm not being fair to you, so I'll just leave." Yet sometimes when you do stay with your experience, you get to a deeper level of what the conflict is really about. It can be intensely painful, but I have found that if a couple can stay with their pain, with awareness, just as I have recommended that individuals stay with their pain, a breakthrough will occur. If you can stay in the impasse for enough time, allowing the difference to exist rather than rushing prematurely to a resolution, you will be changed by the experience. This change is not predictable. It doesn't take the form of giving in or compromising but rather of expanding yourself.

In Paul and Paula's case, after they had stayed with their pain and uncertainty for about six months, they both stated that they felt trans-formed by the experience: Paul discovered that his need for other lovers was actually con-nected to some unresolved anger both at Paula and at his mother. After he was able to express his anger to both women and to get over it, Paul shared: "What I thought I needed for my survival doesn't seem so crucial now." Paula also got a deeper look at herself after staying with her pain about the situation. She remembered a time early in the marriage when Paul broke one of his agreements with her — an agreement that had to do with money, not sex. After she cleared this up with Paul, by expressing her resentment, she then saw that "breaking agreements" had been a button for her all her life. She did some crying and grieving for some of the disappointments she had felt as a child. Afterward, she was finally free enough of old baggage to say truthfully, "I feel a lot safer, like my security doesn't depend on other people, like I'll be okay if the relationship ends, even though I still very much want to be with Paul."

> For many couples just staying in the impasse, holding their differences for a period of time, produces an inner expansion or transformation that enables them to experience a deeper level of what's real for each of them.

Outcomes like this often feel magical or unbelievable to the people involved — when they consider where they were before they got unstuck. For many couples just staying in the impasse, holding their differences for a period of time, produces an inner expansion or transformation that enables them to experience a deeper level of what's real for each of them. I have seen this type of inner transformation occur many times in my career as a coun-selor and coach. I have come to fully trust the process that occurs when you let yourself simply hang out with uncertainty. The result is well worth it.

Staying Present Exercise

To help you experience holding differences, find someone with whom you have unfinished business to do this exercise with you. Pair up and face each other. Partner A opens the dialogue by sharing a resentment about the other partner (using the sentence structure, "I resent you for..." and then sharing bodily sensations, self-talk, or anything else related to the resentment.) Partner B actively listens and then, when his partner says she is satisfied with how he listened to her, shares what he is experiencing right in the moment. He does not respond to the content of her message, unless he frames it as his self-talk. His experience can be whatever he feels, thinks, or says to himself after hearing what A said. Partner A actively listens and then shares her present experience. They keep going back and forth like this for five to ten minutes. Here's an example:

> *Frank:* I resent you for staying home every day, for not having a job that brings in money. I feel a tightness in my jaw and in my throat. And my self-talk, or my judgment, is you're taking it easy while I bust my fanny supporting us.
>
> *Nora:* You resent me for not having a paying job. Your jaw and throat are tight. And your self-talk is that I have it easy while you bust your buns. Is that what you said? (Frank nods.) Okay. I resent you for saying I have an easy life. I feel that in my face, and in my arms and hands. They're tense.
>
> *Frank:* You resent me for saying you have an easy life. Your face and arms and hands feel tense. Did I hear you correctly? (Nora nods.) And I resent you for not offering to go out and get a job. And I didn't say you have an easy life. I said my self-talk is that you're taking it easy.
>
> *Nora:* You're saying you resent me for not offering to go to work. Did I get it?
>
> *Frank:* There was one other thing I said: I didn't say you have

an easy life. My self-talk was that you're taking it easy. I imagine you're taking it easy. Okay?

Nora: You didn't say I have an easy life, you said I'm taking it easy... you imagine. Right? (Frank nods.) And I'm feeling sad. I'm saying to myself that I'm not unwilling to go to work. I'm unsure of myself in the arena that you're so good in.

Frank: You're feeling sad and you're thinking that you don't have confidence in your ability to handle a job. Is that right? (She nods.) And right now I'm feeling softer toward you. I can feel a relaxation in my belly and around my heart.

Nora: You say you're feeling softer toward me. Yes? (He nods.) I feel the tension going out of my face, and I'm feeling a little bit softer and more relaxed now too.

In this example, Frank and Nora started out resenting each other and ended up feeling softer toward each other. Although things don't always happen this way, often they do. I have seen this sort of change happen many times when two people, mated or not, stay present to what the other has just said and share their here-and-now response. Paying careful attention to your own experience and to each other allows for feelings to be experienced more fully so that they can be released. Paying attention also builds a sense of intimacy or connection — even if the disagreement still exists. Married couples, note this point well!

> Paying attention also builds a sense of intimacy or connection — even if the disagreement still exists. Married couples, note this point well!

If you are in a relationship with a long history of conflict, it would be a good idea to do this exercise with another person or pair observing. Having a witness or witnesses helps you stay with the exercise, which can be very difficult. Couples are so used to bypassing their present experience and going immediately into their interpretations, stereotypes, knee-jerk reactions, and self-protective judgments about each other. It's highly unusual for people to simply share their present experience. Frank and Nora's conversation took place between real person and real person instead of between one's interpretation and the other's interpretation. The latter would look more like this: "You don't care about my needs. I've told you a hundred times what I want." (This is an interpretation followed by a generalization. He can't really know what she does or does not care about.) "Well, you don't care about my needs either! You never treat me with respect." (Another interpretation and another generalization.) Does this sound familiar? Well, if you've ever been married for any length of time, I'll bet it does! Mates who have been together for a while tend to camouflage the really painful unfinished situations by making interpretations, generalizations, comparisons, and assessments. They apparently hope that this sort of more distant, less intimate, language will keep them a safe distance from the pain.

> Mates who have been together for a while tend to camouflage the really painful unfinished situations by making interpretations, generalizations, comparisons, and assessments.

Holding differences trains you to tolerate more intensity of feeling, whether it be painful or pleasurable. As a practice it helps you stay with the discomfort, and stay with noticing your experience, until clarity is reached. It also helps partners discover what is real for each other, instead of getting caught up defending their interpretations and stereotypes. Using active listening with the intent of staying in your experience is a very effective tool for helping you stick to *what is,* rather than escaping into explanations or defensiveness.

Holding Differences in a Nutshell

- Differences in viewpoint or desires are inevitable. Learning to allow the differences to exist is a good starting place for healing between people.

- Holding differences gives you the capacity to accept that differences do exist. When you learn to hold two apparently conflicting views side by side, the difference doesn't seem so threatening, your view expands, and often, the contradiction vanishes.
- Active listening is one of the best communication tools for learning to hold differences. Another good tool is observing, with awareness, your own and your partner's differing contact-withdrawal rhythms.
- When you accept that there is no effective way to control what another thinks, and that all attempts at such control simply introduce static into your communication, then you are better prepared to deal with diversity. You can start to value being honest about disagreements and diverse perspectives — because of what you can learn from other people.
- Once you learn to embrace paradox, you see that "all is one," that everything that exists is part of a great universal oneness.
- Life becomes a painful battle when you struggle against *what is,* including differences in perceptions and styles of relating. We create unnecessary suffering when we cannot accept our differences from others and the seemingly contradictory impulses within ourselves. I'll address the apparent contradictions in our inner world in the next chapter.

CHAPTER	SHARING MIXED EMOTIONS

10

YOU'RE NOT CRAZY, YOU'RE COMPLEX

If you have read this far, by now you have probably thought of someone you haven't been completely honest with. I know I have! So take the time to contemplate: How do you feel as you anticipate telling her something that might be difficult to express? Do you notice any mixed feelings — such as a desire to express your feelings and at the same time a fear about her reaction? In my case, a friend and former business partner comes to mind. I want to tell him I resent him for not paying me the money he owes me, but my mind warns me that I could lose his friendship if I upset him. This second thought effectively stops my energy flow. Now, mind you, I know I will have this conversation with him, but even after all these years of practicing the ten truth skills and knowing how well they work, I still have fearful thoughts sometimes. In this case, my mixed feelings are I feel my anger, and I also notice a hesitation that I call fear. I fear that if I tell him my resentment, he might cut off communication with me. What do I do? Do I speak up or shut up?

Well, I'm sure you have guessed from the title of this chapter that my recommendation is to express both things, if you really are feeling both. Practice truth skill #9! I do not recommend disclosing your fear as a strategy for getting the other person's sympathy. If you're being manipulative, you won't get to a feeling of completion about the issue, because a manipulation is not an expression of your present foreground; rather, it's a strategy focused on the future.

As I imagine how the conversation with my friend might start out, here's what I envision: "Bob, I have some unfinished business to clear up with you. Are you available for this conversation? Okay, good. I have a resentment I want to express, and now I'm aware that I'm also feeling something like fear, a fluttering sensation in my stomach. I think the fear is about the fact that I don't want to lose your friendship, and I want to let you know about this resentment because by not expressing it, I'm finding it hard to be around you. I resent you for saying you'd pay me the $10,000 you owe me and then not paying it. I really resent you for that. And I'm still feeling some fear, but less. I resent you for not paying me the money you owe me."

That's it. Afterward I would check in with how I felt and share that too. If I still felt unfinished, I'd repeat my resentment or say it a different way. If I felt complete, I'd tell him that. Then I'd see if he had any response. I'd listen to it and then share whatever I felt after that — resentment, appreciation, and so on.

Self-Assessment Quiz

The following quiz will help you see how skilled you are at expressing mixed emotions. For each statement, rate yourself from 1 to 5, with 1 being generally not true of you and 5 being generally true.

1. I believe it is always better to have one clear feeling than two feelings at the same time.
2. I try to avoid feeling confused.
3. I get impatient with other people who say they feel one thing then right away say they also feel another.

4. It would bother me if people thought of me as uncertain or unsure of myself.

5. If I had to reprimand or discipline someone that I loved, I'd try to keep a stiff upper lip and refrain from showing them my softer, caring feelings.

If you scored several 3's, 4's, and 5's, you may hold such a strong belief about having to be consistent and firm that you may not allow yourself to experience the full range of your feelings. These types of beliefs often interfere with our ability to perceive what we're actually feeling, because we're so busy thinking we shouldn't be feeling all those things in the first place.

Sharing Mixed Emotions with Family

Ken, even though he is in his forties, is living with his parents while he gets his life back together after his divorce. His mother's frequent questioning about how he's doing and where he's going is driving him nuts. He wants to tell her this in the hopes that maybe she'll become aware of what she's doing and stop or that he'll feel less bothered once he expresses what's on his mind. He is also very grateful to his mom and dad for opening their home to him during this time of crisis. He imagines he'd sound ungrateful if he told his mom how much her behavior bothers him. He is genuinely grateful; and her questions do bug him. Both things are true. After attending one of my workshops and learning about this truth skill, he thinks he has found a safe way to speak honestly with his mom. He sees that he could try expressing all his various feelings — his gratitude, his fear of hurting her, and his irritation about the frequency of her questions.

What he decided to do was this: the next time his mom's questions bugged him, he would take the time to identify and feel his feelings instead of focusing so much on what he wished she would do differently. He would notice all his feelings — the caring, appreciative feelings as well as the frustrated, angry feelings. He would also notice his thoughts about having any of those feelings, his self-talk, such as, "I shouldn't be so ungrateful." Then he would reflect on his intent, asking himself, "Am I wanting to clear the air or discover how she feels (relate)? Or am I wanting to get her to stop what she's doing or make her feel bad (control)?" After this, he would go ahead and express his various thoughts and feelings, all strung together just as they occurred inside him. And finally, he would be sure to listen to whatever his mom wanted to say in response. He would not hit and run. He would allow her feelings to affect him and show her how he was affected through his response.

> The way out of confusion is not to fight it but to allow one of your several feelings to float to the foreground and be expressed, even if you also feel something else in the background.

When Ken reported back to me how it had gone with his mom, he expressed surprise that she did not fall apart after hearing his feelings. He was very happy and proud of himself for what he had done and how he had done it. Ken also mentioned that since the confrontation with his mom, he seemed to be better at asserting his boundaries with his girlfriend. In this relationship, he also needed to express some mixed feelings — something along the lines of "I need some alone time right now, and I don't want you to go too far away."

It's Okay to Feel Confused

A workshop participant, Polly, exclaimed, "I'm so confused. I feel too many things at once. I'd better just shut up before I make a complete fool of myself." I often find myself reminding people like Polly that there is nothing shameful about feeling confused. Most self-aware people experience mixed feelings fairly often. Confusion simply means that more than one thing is pulling on your attention. The way

out of confusion is not to fight
it but to allow one of your several feelings to float to the foreground and be expressed, even if
you also feel something else in

Don't use the fact that you are
confused or don't know where to
start as an excuse for not
expressing yourself at all.

the background. Once this is done, see what emerges next in your
foreground, and express that. Usually when you express what's in
your foreground, the way is cleared for the next "layer of the onion"
to be expressed. You will come to trust this process if you can simply
allow it. Don't use the fact that you are confused or don't know where
to start as an excuse for not expressing yourself at all.

Sharing Mixed Emotions with Children

Lars is upset because his fifteen-year-old son, Ted, just seriously
damaged his new power lawn mower while cutting the grass. In fact,
Lars is furious, because money is tight for the family right now, yet
he also appreciates Ted's intent to be helpful around the house. Lars
knows he needs to confront Ted with his feelings. But which feelings
— the anger or the appreciation?

Why not both? Who says you can't appreciate your son's good
intentions while at the same time being angry that he has damaged
something? The fact that Lars can feel both his appreciation and his
anger shows that he is emotionally mature enough to hold two
seemingly conflicting feelings that really are not contradictory at all.
Both make sense as he steps back and looks at the bigger picture.
The ability to do this means that Lars isn't stuck in an immediate
reaction. He has enough perspective on his reactions to realize that
his first impulse may not be the whole story.

So Lars tells Ted, "I want to talk to you about what happened with
the lawn mower." Then, after asking for Ted's views and listening to
what he has to say, Lars says, "I appreciate you for volunteering to do
the lawn. I like that you are helping out more around here. And I

know you were trying to get it all done before the rain. So I know you felt some time pressure. And I also feel really angry and upset that the new mower now needs major repairs. I'm angry at you for not reading the instruction manual or asking me for help before you started work."

Notice that Lars did not say, "I appreciate you, *but* I'm also angry." Using the word *but* in that context would have the effect of canceling whatever came before. He used *and:* "I appreciate you for _____ *and* I resent you for _____." Using *and* instead of *but* sends the message that both parts of the sentence are true. There is great value in including both your feelings in one statement. Sharing both can give your statement added depth and genuineness.

Mixed Feelings in Marriage

Another type of situation in which mixed feelings can arise is when you feel pain for someone else's predicament and pain for yourself. Ava is the major caregiver for her disabled husband, Reese, who cannot walk and spends most of his time in front of the television in his wheelchair. Since Reese's accident, Ava has curtailed most of her social life to work full-time and care for her husband. As the months since the accident grow into years, Ava finds herself feeling sorry for herself more and more frequently. She lets herself notice and experience the pain and recognizes it as a signal that something inside her is not being expressed, that something needs to change. She wants more time away from the house and away from Reese, whom she dearly loves, but whom she is also starting to resent.

She resents Reese's frequent requests for help. She also feels sorrow about the predicament she is in. And she feels genuine empathy for Reese's wishes to have her around to talk to and for the pain he must feel about having lost his ability to walk. Thinking about expressing any of these things scares her. She's afraid of stirring up even more pain. "Haven't we suffered enough?" she rationalizes. But as she stays with her mixture of feelings, she knows that she must express them to Reese. She tells him she wants his undivided attention, so they turn off the television and she begins: "Reese, I'm feeling a pain in my heart for the predicament we're in here. I feel resentment toward you for asking me to stay home this morning. And yet always in the background is how much I love you. I appreciate how you listen to me, and how you look at me when we're together. I really do love your company. And I want to get out of the house more. I want to walk in nature the way we used to. I'm so sad for you that you can't do that anymore."

> There is great value in including both your feelings in one statement. Sharing both can give your statement added depth and genuineness.

This conversation was a good beginning for the pair. After saying those things and seeing that they actually felt closer as a result, she realized she would probably need to do this sort of sharing often. Once was not going to be enough. The situation was not going to change very much on the outside, so she needed to take care of herself on the inside to keep herself from getting stuck. She would keep this conversation alive so that they could become better and better at talking about feelings they found difficult to express and at clearing the air regularly. The truth is, it does get easier.

When to Use This Truth Skill

This truth skill can be useful when your buttons get pushed and you want to let the other person know about it in a nonblaming way. Here's how that might look: start by recalling what the other person did, your reaction, and your feelings or thoughts about that reaction. Disclosing all parts of your response will allow you to improve your skill at sharing mixed emotions. As an example, you might feel anger or jealousy or fear but also wish you had not reacted that way. In this case, share what you are feeling and then add, "and I'm also thinking that I wish I hadn't reacted that way."

Another situation in which you can practice this skill is when you receive surprising feedback. Perhaps you feel upset because someone just gave you some feedback that's different from how you perceive yourself. At the same time, you do want to know how other people see you. You don't want people to walk on eggshells around you. So how do you relate all these things truthfully? You could say, "I resent you for saying I sounded inauthentic. I think I'm feeling misunderstood. And I also have self-talk that says I'm not wanting to cut myself off from getting that type of feedback just because it makes me uncomfortable — so I do appreciate you for telling me I sounded inauthentic."

Any time your response to a situation or to someone else's expression consists of several parts, you have an opportunity to practice expressing mixed emotions. Maybe you have two or more different feelings, as in "I feel scared, and I want to do it anyway." Or you have an immediate reaction tempered by a more considered afterthought,

> Do not assume that one feeling cancels out the other(s). Both (or all) can be true.

as in "Yes, I'll marry you! Well, that's what I feel, but maybe we'd better talk about a few things first." Or maybe you have a feeling followed by a thought or judgment about that feeling as in "I'm jealous! I don't want you to go on that business trip without me, and I'm judging myself for feeling this way. I wish I felt more trusting and less clingy."

As with the other skills, after some conscious practice, you'll probably find yourself sharing mixed feelings more spontaneously and naturally. You won't have to think about it anymore, because the appropriate responses will be there when you need them.

Sharing Mixed Emotions in a Nutshell

- As with the other truth skills, we've seen how important it is to notice *what is* without praise or blame, to be sincere, to stay with feelings without cutting them off, to express what you feel and allow it to change, and to notice your aim.

- Whenever you care for a person but don't like something he's done, you have an opportunity to practice sharing mixed emotions. Other occasions are when you wish to express anger but fear damaging the friendship; when you appreciate the other's intent, even though they fell short on the execution of that intent; when you need to assert your boundaries or wants, while at the same time empathizing with the other; when you have an immediate reaction followed by a more considered response; when you want to do something but are also scared; or when you have one feeling, immediately followed by a thought or judgment about that feeling.

> After communicating something that you imagine is difficult to receive, stay around long enough to hear and deal with the other person's response.

- Start out by sharing whichever feeling or thought is foreground, and then allow the other feeling or feelings to surface and be expressed. Do not assume that one feeling cancels out the other(s). Both (or all) can be true.

- If you appreciate something a person did and also resent something else, start by expressing whichever is in your foreground. Notice whether you feel relaxed or tense. Tension means the resentment is foreground for you, so express that first. Then keep expressing the resentment(s) until your bodily feelings change. When you feel more open and relaxed, and the resentment seems to have faded, share your appreciations.

- After communicating something that you imagine is difficult to receive, stay around long enough to hear and deal with the other person's response.

EMBRACING THE SILENCE OF NOT KNOWING

ENTERING THE FERTILE VOID

Authentic communication depends as much on silence as it does on words — the silences between your words and the silence you leave after you have spoken, awaiting the other's response. Silence is needed to allow your words to sink in. You also hear yourself better when there are silences. Listening to yourself is an essential ingredient for being present. Silence between words also provides room for new ideas and feelings to gestate and take form — yours and the other person's. Becoming comfortable with silence is what truth skill #10, embracing silence, is about. When you can embrace silence, you do not need to know everything in advance or have all the blanks filled in. You understand that there are many things that cannot be known all at once or once and for all. These things emerge gradually as we learn to be more patient and to openly wait, without forcing the issue.

Have you ever noticed how some people (maybe even you!) ask a question and then, before the other person has had a chance to respond, answer it themselves? When I notice myself doing this, I know it's an indication that I'm avoiding something — probably the void. In ancient mythology, the void or the silence was seen as the emptiness out of which all things are created. In all cultures, the void is a powerful symbol. It is the ground of creation, the sea out of which new life emerges. It is also associated with death, the unknown. And for some unknown reason, people tend to fear the unknown.

Just the other day when I was at a friend's house, I noticed she had a bulletin board in her group room with flyers and announcements of coming events. I started to ask if I could post one of my workshop flyers on her board, but as soon as I asked the question, I felt anxiety about how she might react. I knew from a previous conversation that she had other things on her mind, so I began to imagine that my question was an imposition. The truth was I had no idea how she would respond. And there was really no reason to be anxious. But I was. So instead of allowing her to answer my question, I answered it myself. I said something like, "Oh we don't have to deal with this now," thus staying in control and avoiding the truth of the present moment, the truth of staying for a few moments in the silence of not-knowing. This mundane example shows how the ego-mind works. If it gets the tiniest bit uncomfortable, it initiates a control pattern — in this case the pattern of filling the silence to avoid feeling the anxiety of waiting for an unknown reply.

> In all cultures, the void is a powerful symbol. It is the ground of creation, the sea out of which new life emerges.

I remember my dad used to do this too. Right after he died, my brothers and I were watching some of the videotapes of television shows he'd been on — as part of our grieving process, as a way to remember him. We had a few tapes of shows in which he had interviewed famous authors about their writings. In one particular segment, he was interviewing Jerome Frank about his book on the nuclear age. He asked, "Dr. Frank, what do you think about the Star

Wars project that our government is putting so much money into?" Then, apparently feeling anxious or uneasy, or wanting the interview to go *his* way, he immediately went on without a pause, "Don't you think it's obvious that this is a manipulation by the military-industrial powers to keep their budgets well funded?" He said a few more things before he finally shut up and let the expert speak. "Dad's answering his own question," quipped my brother Al. We all got a good laugh out of that. It felt so familiar to us all.

Sometimes Nothing Is Better Than Something

When I was thirteen years old and just getting interested in boys, I used to engage regularly in another practice that is actually the opposite of embracing silence. If I knew that a boy was planning to call me on a particular night, I would jot down a page of notes about subjects to talk about if the conversation started to lag and cute quips to come back with if he said what I thought he was going to say. I had my part all scripted! I thought doing this made me appear confident and cool, and I believed that it would also put the boy at ease — you know, no long awkward silences. Maybe it did make me look cool, but I doubt that it put the boy at ease. I imagine it made for a pretty stiff, unreal conversation. And I now know that looking cool is not the purpose of life!

When I reflect on my teenage need to be ready with a quick comeback, I recognize two rather strongly held cultural beliefs: the belief that something is better than nothing and the idea that fast is better than slow. Are we ready to challenge these outdated notions? Are we ready to enter the realm of uncertainty together so that we can experience true in-the-moment contact?

> The belief that knowing is better than not knowing is one of the fundamental dysfunctional beliefs of our culture.

The belief that knowing is better than not knowing is one of the fundamental dysfunctional beliefs of our culture. Somewhere we got the idea that our emotional security depends on being able to control how we come across to others. *Not knowing* makes us feel not in control. Thinking we know, even if what we "know" is not true, makes us feel on top of things. When we're operating from this perspective, we think that if we act knowledgeable or say the right thing, people will think better of us. What we forget is that this sort of control is an illusion.

Self-Assessment Quiz

Here's a quiz to help you assess your ability to tolerate silence, empty space, or not knowing. For each question, rate yourself from 1 to 5 (with 1 being not usually true of you and 5 being mostly true):

1. I often finish people's sentences for them (or at least I feel like doing it).
2. I find it frustrating when someone takes a long time to make his point.
3. If someone asks me a question, I usually answer it right away, without much reflection.
4. If I ask someone else a question, I like her to answer it right away and not leave me hanging.
5. I sometimes ask a question and then answer it myself without giving the other a chance to reply.
6. I find it hard to tolerate ambiguity, uncertainty, or being in limbo.
7. When I'm around the house alone, I often keep radio, television, or music playing in the background.
8. I like to keep busy (or, even if I don't think I like it, I usually am busy).

If you scored several 3's, 4's, or 5's, embracing silence is probably a challenge for you. In this doing-oriented culture, we do not learn to value silence. In school we were taught that knowing is better than not knowing. And on the job, looking busy is generally preferred to sitting at your desk staring out the window.

The most important thing about embracing silence in a human interaction is that it allows for feelings to be fully experienced, your inner feelings and the feelings being exchanged. This helps you develop your ability to notice *what is* and prepares you to communicate with more of your whole being, so you're not just coming from your head or your automatic control pattern. I recommend that you pause before speaking — to check in with yourself, to get grounded in your bodily sensations, and to connect with the other person. This takes a few seconds of silence. During this silence, energy is building to support the contact between you and the other.

> I recommend that you pause before speaking — to check in with yourself, to get grounded in your bodily sensations, and to connect with the other person.

Embracing Silence in Groups

Notice your behavior the next time you are sharing in a group setting: Do you begin talking right away, as soon as it's your turn? Or do you take a few seconds to connect? Do you have something planned to say before you begin to address the group? Or do you sit in the silence and see what emerges?

To encourage the people in my groups to allow time to connect with themselves and others before speaking, I often use the "talking egg" — a toy egg that gets passed to whomever is speaking next, signifying that it's her turn to speak and that no one can interrupt, even if she's sitting in silence. In the Native American Indian tradition, when people sit in a circle, they use the "talking stick" to signify whose turn it is to speak. I find that using the talking egg supports people in embracing silence. They can hold the egg for a while before opening their mouth. This gives them a chance to check in and feel how they feel before they start talking. Likewise, at the end of their sharing, they can hold the egg as long as they wish, so they can really make contact with the others and take in their response instead of rushing offstage as soon as they've finished speaking.

In many group meetings that I attend, everyone seems to be competing for air time. At the briefest pause in conversation, someone will jump in to get her piece in — even if the previous speaker was simply pausing for breath. In our fast-paced culture, we've learned that we'd better not breathe too much or we'll lose our turn! This is why I use the talking egg in my groups — as an antidote to this tendency to rush in to fill every void.

Allowing for silences between sharings seems to help people become present before they speak. As a result, the things that are said seem more real.

The Quakers use a practice in their meetings that encourages listening to the silence of one's own inner truth before speaking. It is the simple practice of only speaking when the spirit moves you. Typically, Quaker meetings are characterized by long silences between the members' thoughtful sharings. I have always felt nourished and inspired by this practice. At times, in my groups, I will describe how a Quaker meeting is run and suggest that we follow those guidelines. Allowing for silences between sharings seems to help people become present before they speak. As a result, the things that are said seem more real.

Take Your Applause

Lee Glickstein, founder of Speaking Circles, a training program for professional speakers, places a lot of emphasis on the importance of silence. In his workshops, he encourages speakers to stand on the stage and look around, making eye contact with a few audience members, one at a time, before they start their speeches. Then, at the end, he tells them, "Stand still. Don't hurry to get off the stage. Take your applause." The speakers who have worked with Lee, and I am one of them, report that after adopting his methods, they feel much more at home onstage and much more connected to their audiences, and they experience much less stage

> After you say something, pause and take in the fact that the other is now receiving what you just said.

fright. I think I feel less fear because this practice allows me to feel connected to myself and others, that is, more present, so the world feels like a friendlier place.

I love Lee's phrase "take your applause," because I find it applies to almost any conversation between people. After you say something, pause and take in the fact that the other is now receiving what you just said. Take in that sense of being received. If you're worried about not being heard, as many people are, this act could be very healing for you.

Embracing Silence Using Meditation

Tanya was a nonstop talker. Her husband, Greg, was more the silent type. Tanya was often frustrated by his lack of attentiveness and reluctance to engage. As the years went by, Tanya seemed to get more demanding, and Greg seemed to get more withdrawn as their differences became more and more polarized. She saw this polarization as a classic case of one partner acting out the shadow of the other, but she was stymied about how to change herself. Then one night, after reading a book about meditation, Tanya decided to try it. Meditation involves sitting still and silent with a straight spine and eyes closed. It occurred to her that this practice might help her marriage and that she had something important to learn from embracing silence — even though the act of sitting quietly was a big stretch for her. Tanya began to sit in meditation for thirty minutes each day, just after getting out of bed in the morning. Greg knew she was doing it, and since it didn't seem to affect his life much, he just let her do her thing.

After practicing meditation for about three months, Tanya began to feel quieter and more spacious inside. It was as if there were more room inside her to notice and feel her feelings, to be aware of her surroundings, and to be more available to whatever was going on. At first she thought, "This is working! And it feels pretty good." But after a few months more, something unexpected happened. Every time she sat in silence, she would notice unpleasant, painful sensations and emotions — a combination of fear, anger, and raw gut pain. "It wasn't supposed to be like this," she complained to herself. "Meditation is supposed to make you more peaceful."

As she continued to meditate, the pain became more persistent and intense. At that point she came to me for counseling, since I was familiar with meditation. I encouraged her to stay with the painful feelings as the noticer, to feel them fully to discover the message in the pain. As she continued meditating and staying with her feelings, she had a vivid memory of being physically abused by her parents when she was four years old. When she bothered them with her demands, they would tie her to a chair in her room with duct tape. These memories horrified her, as she wondered if staying with the pain was really the right thing to do. Working with me, Tanya learned to support her wounded inner child from the place of loving spaciousness that she had discovered within herself. She also realized that she needed to get completion with her parents, both of whom were still alive but who were now quite aged. She made a date to meet with them, hoping to use some of

> It was as if there were more room inside her to notice and feel her feelings, to be aware of her surroundings, and to be more available to whatever was going on.

the truth skills she had been learning with me. Her intent was to let them see the feelings she had gotten in touch with during meditation so she could heal herself and her relationship with them. She had some fear about expressing her anger at what they had done, because she imagined it would upset them. And she was committed to listening to their response, to actively listen or hold differences if needed. But, in essence, she was more committed to truth than to safety, so she called her parents and arranged for a meeting. On the phone, she told them that she had begun meditating, and that sitting in silence had allowed her to listen more deeply to some things she had repressed about her childhood. She did not give them the details over the phone. I generally recommend that you save the details for the face-to-face meeting.

When the meeting occurred, she started out by describing the resentments and appreciations process, as discussed in chapter 3. She told them her intent was to get over the anger and pain she felt about some things they had done to her when she was a child. Her intent was not to hurt or punish them. She had heard that this sort of frank conversation could lead to forgiveness, and she felt she had to try it. She said that she wanted them to simply listen until she had finished, and then she would like to listen to them. She began by sitting quietly, just looking at them. Then she expressed her resentments one by one to each of them: "Dad, I resent you for sitting me in that chair and tying me in with duct tape when I was four years old." "Mom, I resent you for helping Dad tie me up with duct tape when I was four years old." "Dad, I resent you for telling me to stop crying when you were tying me up with duct tape!" She continued with her resentments as they came to her, often repeating them just so she could feel her feelings more clearly.

After about twenty-five minutes of sharing resentments, she remembered some things she was grateful for. So she expressed these too: "Dad, I appreciate you for saying you were sorry after you spanked me that time when I was five. I appreciate you for teaching me to read. I appreciate you for telling me I was smart." She spent about ten minutes expressing her appreciations to both her mom and dad. By the time it was their turn to speak, they were all crying. Both her parents expressed sincere sorrow at the pain they had inflicted on her. They sheepishly asked for her forgiveness and were elated when Tanya said she felt she could now let go of the anger and the pain. Before this conversation, Tanya had only spoken to her parents at Christmas and on birthdays for the past twelve years. She knew she had been feeling alienated from them, but she hadn't had the free attention to look honestly at what she was withholding. She had chosen instead to go into denial about her feelings, using non-stop talking as one of her avoidance patterns.

When she returned, she told me she felt stronger and clearer than she had ever felt. "And now I have parents — parents that I really like and love — in spite of the awful things they did. I survived. I'm okay. I think I'm more okay for having gone through that difficult childhood and coming out the other end. I have learned some lessons about pain and healing that I may need to use again in the future."

> Every human interaction entails a large measure of uncertainty. Each time you express yourself, you take a step into the unknown, into "empty space."

Tanya had been in therapy before, but not until she became a meditator could she be still enough to access the really deep memories that she had been running from. After she completed with her parents, her compulsion to talk all the time seemed to vanish. She now realized that Greg actually does say quite a bit. He just speaks quietly and slowly. She had never noticed this about him before, because she wasn't able to listen. She was always either talking out loud or to herself. As you might imagine, her marriage also improved after the visit with her parents. Now it was Greg's turn to get an earful! But that's another story. Let me just say that they survived just fine.

Using Uncertainty to Connect

Every human interaction entails a large measure of uncertainty. Each time you express yourself, you take a step into the unknown, into "empty space." When Tanya started telling her dad what she resented, she had no idea how he would respond. She was taking a risk on behalf of the relationship. I imagine her dad sensed the courage that took, even if he didn't like what he was hearing.

Any time you express yourself to someone, you may be trying to remain unattached to the outcome, but you probably do care what the other's response will be. But you can't know what it will be, you'll be in limbo, until he shares it with you. So while you're waiting for a response, see if you can embrace the silence. Feel your own feelings as you listen and wait. Allow the sense of connection to build. Don't speak and then immediately disconnect as soon as you have spoken. Stay with the energy of connection for a while. If you find yourself using a control pattern to avoid these moments of uncertainty with others, you could "go out and come in again," as discussed in chapter 8. It's never too late to revise or redo an interaction as long as the people involved are still alive.

> Allow the sense of connection to build. Don't speak and then immediately disconnect as soon as you have spoken. Stay with the energy of connection for a while.

But what if you are attached to the outcome? What if you not only *care* about the other's response, but you can't stand to be told no or to be disagreed with? If you do "care too much," if you are impatient or attached to a certain outcome, it will be difficult for you to embrace silence. You may feel compelled to fill in the empty space between your expression and her response with more words of your own. When my dad was interviewing Jerome Frank, he probably wanted to make sure he got an answer he could work with — so he answered his question himself. If you imagine that someone may not give you the response you want, you may go into whatever control pattern you use for such situations, some kind of sales pitch, perhaps. But doing so creates static rather than connection between you. As a result, you may never discover what the other person really thinks or feels. If you're not able to be still and receptive, the other will sense that you're not open, so he won't offer his deepest and truest expression. He may just tell you what he thinks you want to hear.

Do You Ask or Do You Tell?

If you want to be the type of person with whom people can be true and honest, if you don't just want to be told what others think you want to hear, take a look at how spacious you are as opposed to how attached you are to getting things to go your way. Think about your recent interactions with people. Notice what proportion of the time you spent telling people what to do, how to do it, or what you think, feel, or want and what proportion you spent asking about their thoughts, feelings, ideas, or wants and then really listening with an open mind. Do you tell or do you ask? Do you take space or do you make space?

If you spend most of your interactive energy on the telling side of the equation, this usually signals a high need to feel in control. If you are in a management role (or a parenting role) in which you need to direct others' efforts, a certain amount of control may be necessary. But there is a way to give assignments that is clear about your expectations and that still leaves room for the other's response and input. You can let the other know that you see it as part of your job to let them know your expectations, clearly

In today's Information Age...we need to know that our information is free from distortions caused by peoples' control patterns and fears about telling it like it is.

and directly. Then you can ask them for feedback on your management style. Find out if it works for them. You can also use some of the tools from chapter 9, "Holding Differences," like presenting your request or viewpoint and then hearing how they see it, using active listening.

Are You Open or Closed?

If someone disagrees with your position on an important matter, do you quickly reassert your position, as in, "Perhaps you didn't hear what I said," or do you inquire about their reasons for their position, as in, "Can you tell me more about why you think that?" This latter response shows people that you are open.

By being open I mean showing that you sincerely seek to learn something from another person. When you have an inquiring attitude, with or without actually asking a question, people can see that you are open to them. They feel significant. They feel safe, so they are more likely to tell it like it is. Your communication is free of static, so the information you get is more likely to be valid. And in today's Information Age, when we base our decisions almost solely on information coming from other people, we need to know that it is free from the distortions caused by people's control patterns and fears about telling it like it is.

Spacious Listening

Embracing silence and being open to listening to others are prerequisites for real, vital human connection. But another type of listening is just as important as listening to others, and that is listening to ourselves, sensing the silences between our words or thoughts. Often the deepest truths arise from the spaces in between words, that fertile void where thoughts are absent.

As a professional speaker, I am asked a lot of questions. Sometimes I acknowledge the question and begin to answer. Then I remember to pause. Sometimes, during the pause, a new feeling arises, something that may appear unrelated to what I have just started to say. If this occurs, I share this response as well, mentioning that I am allowing my thinking process to be transparent so they can see how I give birth to an idea. To the control-oriented mind, my response could sound unpolished or half-baked. Then I pause again, and a clearer message comes out, one that ties the two seemingly unrelated thoughts together. My response took a bit of time and space to form into something coherent.

> Often the deepest truths arise from the spaces in between words, that fertile void where thoughts are absent.

Human communication is an alive, ever-changing creation — it is created, re-created, and cocreated in each moment. And creation requires patience: the ability to tolerate emptiness.

Trusting the Silence Exercise

Having an open, inquiring attitude requires the ability to tolerate not knowing and not being in control of where the conversation will end up. As you learn to let go of control, you learn to trust yourself to consider another person's views without losing your own (holding differences) and to be okay even when you have nothing to say (embracing silence).

Profound things happen when two people sit face-to-face and openly explore their feelings toward each other in the present. In my workshops, there are often moments when two people are beginning to engage in dialogue and then one or both will quickly escape from genuine contact by going into a story or a theory, only tangentially related to the here and now. That's when I go into action as their embracing silence coach. I ask Partner A to state a feeling she is experiencing in relation to Partner B. Then, before B can escape into a story or a theory, I request that B simply pause, take in what A shared, and then check in with himself to see what he is experiencing right now, and share that.

Then A does the same thing — listen, pause, check in, feel, and then respond genuinely to B about how she is feeling right now, not two minutes ago. The beauty of this exercise is it shows how feelings change from moment to moment. If you give yourself the space to feel and express *what is* now, *what is* in the next moment will usually be different. In addition to helping people learn to be more comfortable with silence, this exercise also helps them get more comfortable with change. Ask someone you know to try this exercise with you. Sit face-to-face and take turns sensing the space between you, speaking from the silence about how you are feeling right now in relationship to the other. In responding to the other, be with your present experience of what was just said to you. Stay with this experience and respond to what you just heard and what you're feeling as a result.

> Human communication is an alive, ever-changing creation — it is created, re-created, and co-created in each moment. And creation requires patience: the ability to tolerate emptiness.

This is similar to the pair exercise I mentioned in chapter 9, in which Partners A and B take turns actively listening and sharing what the other's sharing triggers in them. In these situations, the conversation is completely spontaneous. No one has a plan for how it should go. Both people are open to being surprised, not just by the other, but by themselves as well. I always feel moved as I witness two people listening into and embracing silence. I can feel their tentativeness, their excitement, their aliveness.

When partners do this exercise, their communications tend to arise from a deep level of their being, showing that you can be uncertain of where you are going and still radiate presence. In fact, people seem more present in these moments, perhaps because the situation demands a high level of open attentiveness. In these moments of heightened spontaneity, people also embody a sense of confidence, or self-trust, that I rarely see in more controlled settings. The willingness to just be here with another person, not knowing the outcome, opens up vast new possibilities — unpredictable and uncontrollable. As we learn to trust the silence, we learn to trust the unknown and the chaotic, which I suspect are where true creativity springs from. From my own experience, I know that when I'm feeling creative, I'm feeling confident.

If people are unable to do this practice, as often occurs with married couples, it may be because there's too much unfinished business between them for them to be able to be present. Then it's time to do resentments and appreciations or one of the other clearing practices.

Are we ready to simply be together in the mystery of not knowing what's coming next, like the two partners facing each other without a script? Can we tolerate the silence and stillness — and the slowness? If we really want to be present in the moment, we'll have to learn to slow down and pay attention to what's bubbling up in our awareness right now. We'll need to get comfortable with the discomfort of not knowing and simply wait to see what comes, even if we feel awkward. Remember, when you're feeling uncertain or unsure about what's coming next, you can be pretty sure that you're in touch with present reality.

Practices to Support Embracing Silence

I have a few other favorite practices for helping myself and others get more comfortable with the silence of not-knowing: word fasting, partying without words, free association, and meditation.

1. *Word fasting.* Sometimes if a friend and I plan to spend the day together, we will agree to be totally silent the whole time. One of the things I like to do best while on a word fast is to take a long hike in a beautiful natural setting. Looking at each other, touching, pointing, laughing, and any form of nonverbal contact is permitted, but no talking, no writing notes in the sand, no sign language. This kind of contact can be a wonderful thing to experience with someone you care about. After the day is over, you may have a conversation about how it felt.

> Profound things happen when two people sit face-to-face and openly explore their feelings toward each other in the present.

2. *Partying without words.* I occasionally invite some of my friends over for an improvisational movement and dance party. It is agreed beforehand that while they are in my home, no one will speak. All forms of nonverbal contact are allowed and encouraged. This practice is similar to word fasting, except that now you're with a group, and there's music to move and dance to. None of the music I play has any audible lyrics.

3. *Free association.* Usually I do this practice with just one other person, but it could be done with a few people. It is modeled after the free-association technique used by Freud and other psychoanalysts since Freud. The two of us lie on a bed or on the floor in a comfortable nest of pillows and blankets that we have created for the occasion. We just lie there, maybe looking at one another, but not

necessarily. When something to say bubbles up from either of our subconsciouses, we speak it aloud. It could be something related to the present situation, or it could be a memory, a feeling, a thought, a wish, a dream fragment, or a theory. You share anything and everything that enters your mind, uncensored. We allow plenty of spaces between the sharings, and no effort is made to have a conversation — although if conversation happens, that's okay too. The experience is a little like a Quaker meeting lying down!

4. *Meditation.* Meditation is usually practiced alone, but you can also do it with a group or with just one or two others. There are many traditions of meditation, such as Zen, Vipassana, and Transcendental (TM). There are also a number of acceptable postures, including sitting, standing, and walking. I will not attempt to describe meditation here, but I do include a number of resources for learning this practice in appendix A, "Resource Guide."

I recommend using these practices often as a way of tuning in to your essential being and your ability to perceive things as they are. Most people get so caught up in the ego-mind's ideation and strategizing that they truly have lost touch with reality. I had a meeting a few weeks ago with a client, Lonnie, who was talking about how she wanted a more intimate connection with her husband. I asked Lonnie to put her husband, metaphorically, in the empty chair across from her and to tell him her feelings and desires. As I listened — and we tape recorded the conversation so she could hear herself too — I realized that 90 percent of what she said was not what she wanted. It was why she wanted it, why she thought it would be good for them, why she didn't want to bother him with her needs — why, why, why, should, should, should. There was very little concrete picture, feeling tone, or description of what she was proposing. As I sat there imagining being her husband listening to her words, I imagined him tuning out about 90 percent of what she said. Lonnie imagined this too when she listened to the tape. She recognized that the whys and shoulds felt safer to her and that her desire for safety was killing her spontaneity.

When she was faced with expressing her wants, Lonnie's control pattern was to overexplain and justify instead of simply saying what she wanted. After we did some work to help reveal to her the false beliefs at work in her unconscious, I recommended that she and her husband engage in the free-association technique to help Lonnie allow some silences between her words. I hoped this practice would help her unhook from the patterned way she expressed herself, that it would give her a chance to slow down and notice when her false beliefs about "being a bother" crept in. For a few weeks, they did this practice at least once a week. Lonnie also listened to the tape recording of her initial conversation with the empty chair a few times — just to help her to be more aware of her control pattern.

> Words themselves are not the problem but rather the unconscious way we use words in the service of our control patterns.

As a result of doing these things, she got in contact with a deeper level of her truth, the level that has clear wants that do not need to be camouflaged by explanations and apologies. Then she and I did another empty-chair dialogue with her husband. This time she was about 70 percent concrete and specific. She was now able to show him, or take him there, with her words. Her picture included specifics like: "I see us taking walks in nature and looking at the birds and listening to them sing. I see us sitting quietly at the kitchen table and looking into each other's eyes."

Recalling this story, I am reminded that words themselves are not the problem but rather the unconscious way we use words in the service of our control patterns. Practices such as word fasting and free association can help you interrupt your patterned way of using words and learn to honor the silences between them.

Embracing Silence in a Nutshell

- When you pause and allow silences between your words, you become more present. You allow deeper levels of truth to emerge from your subconscious.
- Embracing silence gives you a chance to fully experience what you feel and to fully take in what you are hearing.
- Pause before speaking — to check in with yourself, to get grounded in your bodily sensations, and to connect with the other. During this silence, energy is building to support the contact between you.
- Take your applause.
- Try the Quaker-meeting format in a group you belong to.
- Practice meditation regularly to help you learn to be still within. This practice opens up channels of listening to yourself that you would not otherwise be sensitive to.
- Notice how often you ask and how often you tell, how often you make space and how often you take space. A balance of both is best.
- Help your mind learn to tolerate and value silence by practicing word fasting and free association with a partner.
- To really make contact with another person, you must be willing to enter into a realm of uncertainty together. Be willing to become unattached to what's coming next, to embrace uncertainty, ambiguity, and even potential chaos.

SERENITY, PRESENCE, AND COMPASSION

12

Now that you know what the ten truth skills are and how to practice them, this chapter will describe the payoff — what you will get for your efforts if you commit yourself to the practice of Getting Real.

Serenity, presence, and *compassion* are the three words that best describe the qualities we begin to embody when we Get Real. Serenity refers to the calmness and inner peace that come from knowing you are okay, no matter what happens to you. Presence is the energetic aliveness and attentiveness that say you're open and available for anything that life may bring. Compassion is your ability to be moved or touched by others' real misfortune or suffering without becoming dramatic or sentimental and without needing to find fault or blame.

When I experience serenity, presence, and compassion in a unified way, my body and mind feel completely relaxed, and yet I have an open attentiveness to my surroundings that enables me to be immediately responsive if need be. I feel a relaxed attentiveness alongside a sense of harmony or unity with the world. I am not identified with my personality or my personal story, but I am able to use these to connect with the world in whatever ways feel most whole and truthful at the time.

Serenity

Throughout this book, I have referred to the ego-mind's need to control. When you are operating from this need, you think things have to be a certain way before you can feel okay. When you're in this mind-set, you will not experience serenity. Your peace of mind will be constantly threatened, because, after all, so many things are not in your control. On the other hand, when you are open to experiencing and learning from everything — every disappointment, every surprise, and every piece of feedback, whether laudatory or critical — then you cannot be threatened. When your priority is to be open to using *what is* for your spiritual evolution, you will see the genuine benefit of every situation you encounter — because no matter what happens, you always learn something from it. You really can't lose!

As you grow in your capacity to experience *what is,* you stop trying to manipulate reality to conform to your comfort zone. You more easily accept your thoughts, your actions, and your circumstances. You take life as it comes. On this Getting Real journey, you come to identify yourself as the noticer or witness of your thoughts and actions instead of being identified with your social roles, your accomplishments, or your ideas about yourself.

> When you are open to experiencing and learning from everything — every disappointment, every surprise, and every piece of feedback, whether laudatory or critical — then you cannot be threatened.

This witness consciousness is an internal point of focus or inner spaciousness. You hold a space with your attention, and many things occur within that space. You sense a consistency in your essential being that stays with you, no matter what is happening in your external world or in your mind. This sense of your essential being is not easily threatened, allowing you to feel peaceful and serene. As noticer or witness, you are open to experiencing *what is*. Nothing needs to be excluded. You do not take sides. If your mind is comparing, judging, or taking sides, the witness notices this. Serenity comes from identifying, not with the push-pulls or ups and downs of your external circumstances or fluctuating emotional states, but with

> Serenity comes from identifying, not with the push-pulls or ups and downs of your external circumstances or fluctuating emotional states, but with consciousness itself.

consciousness itself. You "become" the stream, not the cork bobbing along in the current of the stream.

If the control freak in you likes feeling on top of things, try shifting your identity to that of the noticer, and you will really be on top of things! But, of course, it won't matter very much, because there's nothing to prove, nothing to defend against, nothing to get on top of. Serenity comes when you are not depending on getting your way to feel good. Your happiness becomes unconditional. No one and nothing can take away your ability to be aware and accepting in the moment. The choice to accept or resist the moment is entirely up to you. Once you trust that you are in charge of your inner state, you can stop worrying about something happening to disturb your peace of mind.

Another theme related to serenity discussed throughout this book is that if you express what is in your foreground, it will soon change. Knowing this, you do not confuse a particular emotional state with who you are. Nor do you need to fear that something terrible will happen if you share your emotions. You trust your moment-to-moment ebb and flow. Thoughts and emotions come and they go. No matter what you are experiencing, it will change.

As you practice experiencing *what is,* you attain more perspective; you see from a wider vantage point. You discover that jobs, money, admirers, possessions, good moods, bad moods, lucky breaks, failures, and misfortune come and go. Anything you have today may be gone tomorrow. Anything you don't have could appear at any time. Experiencing *what is* helps you draw a bigger circle around the ups and downs of your existence. The ups and the downs are not separate. Together they comprise your life, your hero's journey. A broader, more inclusive perspective tends to even things out, to mitigate the extremes, to unify the opposites.

When you become better at noticing and sharing your self-talk, you get perspective on your mind chatter. You see that it isn't right or wrong. It just is. You come to accept it without praise or blame. You learn to share it, partly in the interest of transparency, partly as a way of help-

> Experiencing what is helps you draw a bigger circle around the ups and downs of your existence.

ing you stay in the present as the noticer or witness, and partly as a way of getting completion. Taking the broader perspective of the noticer helps you take challenges and unwanted surprises in stride.

As you learn to accept *what is,* you become more able to let other people have their reactions to you — positive, negative, or neutral. Your sense of safety becomes internal — something nobody can take away. You are more self-trusting, knowing you aren't dependent on others to make you feel safe.

Experiencing *what is,* being transparent, sharing mixed feelings, holding differences, welcoming feedback, asserting what you want and don't want, and embracing silence all support serenity, because they bring you into the present moment. You are connecting and relating to more of what there is to feel related to. The more connected you are to yourself, to others, or to the situation, the greater will be your overall sense of well-being.

Presence

The greatest gift you can give yourself and others is your free, open attention: your presence. Although presence as a concept is somewhat intangible, when you are truly present, you can feel it energetically, and so can others. As you become more spacious and more able to attend to what is happening within your current awareness, you become more present. Presence begins with attention. You have all your energy and attention available to you as the noticer, so you can participate fully in each moment of your life.

I think most of us miss too many of our present moments. Many of us are tied to the past, reliving or trying to live down old fears. Others of us tend to get ahead of ourselves, focusing more on how we want things to turn out than on being open to each moment as it comes. Mostly, we run away from the uncertainty and aliveness of the present moment by thinking about it (assessing it, judging it, comparing it to something else, planning how to get it to last) instead of experiencing it.

The more aware you are of your actual experience in each moment, the more present you are. You may become aware that you are not very present, that you are distracted by your judgments or other mind chatter, or that you are caught up in a story based on the past. Through learning to notice your mind chatter or self-talk, you always have a way of getting back into present time.

> Presence begins with attention. You have all your energy and attention available to you as the noticer, so you can participate fully in each moment of your life.

Another way of affirming your presence is to notice and share your intent as a part of your message. For example, when Dana says, "I'm going to tell you a bit of my story about past relationships before I say what's going on now," it's easier for us to listen to her story. We know that she is aware of what she is doing. And by sharing in this

> Through learning to notice your mind chatter or self-talk, you always have a way of getting back into present time.

way, she is giving us credit for being aware also.

To be present, you need to be *relating* to what is happening now — in this situation, with this person, in your current state. A very important aspect of your current state is your foreground, whatever is uppermost in your awareness. When you try to suppress a thought or feeling or to push it into the background, your demeanor will give you away. Your communication won't be congruent. You'll be saying, "I'm doing great!" while slumping and looking down at the ground or "I have no problem with what you're saying" in a voice that sounds angry. The self-awareness that comes from practicing the ten truth skills helps you notice when your words and actions don't jibe. As you Get Real, you will come to take for granted that we're all pretty transparent in our incongruities. You also learn these giveaways are no big deal. All you need to do is admit that you notice them, and that brings you present again.

Your mental habits are what keep you from being present — habits like making judgments, having expectations, and filling in the blanks. Honest communication about any of these things always brings you back into the present. So if you notice yourself going into an automatic self-criticism pattern, for example, share your self-talk about noticing this. This will bring you back to now. By letting go of the need to be right, safe, and certain in favor of being real, unique, and open to surprise, you affirm yourself as a living, ever-changing presence — participating in life's changes instead of trying to control them. As such a presence, you are in constant and immediate exchange with the world and the people around you — always in flux, always in relationship. You are energetically alive. People can feel you when you come into a room. When you look at them, they feel seen. When you listen, they feel heard. When you speak, they listen.

Only when you become unattached to how others behave or how life treats you can you be truly present. A circle of mutual causality is at work here, because it is also true that the more present you are, the easier it is to let go of such attachments. But as with any new skill, practice is essential. So be grateful for those moments of presence, and keep practicing.

Compassion

Compassion comes from feeling connected to others. It allows you to experience, accept, and love *what is*. When you are fully self-expressed, and at one with yourself, you tend to feel at one with others also. There is little or no sense of separation. So if I am saying something which I imagine may be painful for you to hear, I sense our connection as I express it. Then the interaction can be a shared experience of two people feeling together rather than a right-wrong or attack-defend situation.

As we saw from the group exercise in chapter 3, in which people share their darkest secrets, your compassion grows as you become more honest about your darker, hidden aspects, the traits you find shameful, the actions you don't want others to know about. And paradoxically, as you accept these darker parts through compassion for yourself, they tend to be influenced and come into alignment with the more beneficial aspects of your nature. They are transformed by the light.

You also need compassion when relating to the wounded inner child — yours and other

> Through being transparent, you learn that you are most lovable when you are most transparent — that people want to love you if you will just let yourself be seen. And maybe, if you let yourself be seen fully by yourself, you'll find an equal willingness within to forgive and to love.

people's. As I have often repeated, you're big now. But you carry inside the conditioned fears and beliefs of your childhood. You don't

You don't have to protect others — because you have learned that being honest is the best way to stay connected to others, to your own flow, and ultimately to that greater energy source from which you both partake.

need to be protected from the truth, but you do need to be treated with kindness when the truth hurts, even if that hurt is only a pain in the ego.

Through being transparent, you learn that you are most lovable when you are most transparent — that people want to love you if you will just let yourself be seen. And maybe, if you let yourself be seen fully by yourself, you'll find an equal willingness within to forgive and to love. When we look honestly at our feelings and thoughts, many people notice harsh judgments about themselves and others. You become compassionate by embracing everything, even your judgments. You embrace your ego-centered mind chatter, your inner critic, your attachments. Accepting your taboo thoughts and feelings is a powerful act of compassion toward yourself, especially those "spiritually incorrect" thoughts about how other people should be. When you share your self-talk about your judgments in a spirit of "confession," of being transparent, you take the sting out of it.

Your compassion will grow as you practice Getting Real with like-minded friends, friends who agree to learn in public, trusting that all mistakes or awkwardness will be forgiven and often celebrated. Even anger and resentment can be shared with compassion. As you share these feelings, you feel your connection to the other, your caring. You don't have to protect others — because you have learned that being honest is the best way to stay connected to others, to your own flow, and ultimately to that greater energy source from which you both partake.

Using the Ten Truth Skills

I hope you are feeling safer now about living your life a bit closer to the edge. The world needs your truth and your aliveness. It needs more people who truly participate in life and take responsibility instead of sitting on the sidelines criticizing or complaining. If you are ready to change the rules of the game you play by, here are some things you can do:

1. Give a copy of this book to at least one friend.
2. Discuss with them the idea of practicing the truth skills with each other.
3. Send for the Getting Real Card Game, and invite your friends over to play it with you. This is a safe, fun way to begin the conversation about "changing the rules of the game." You'll find a description of the game, including sample questions and ordering information, in appendix C.
4. Trust yourself. Leap joyfully into the unknown!

Getting Real in a Nutshell

- Getting Real keeps your energy moving. You'll feel more alive after practicing the ten truth skills, because your life energy will be flowing, not constricted and confined.
- Getting Real keeps relationships alive. Practicing the ten truth skills keeps your relationships from becoming stagnant. You get in the habit of expressing and releasing instead of holding on to grievances. When partners store up withheld feelings, a wall grows between them that can only be broken down by getting the energy moving again through self-expression.
- Getting Real sets you free. When you know how to notice and stay with an uncomfortable experience, you have true freedom. You are not compelled by your conditioning to need things to be a certain way for you to feel okay. You are not controlled by your need to avoid certain feared outcomes.
- Getting Real creates a shift in your identity. Your ability to identify yourself as the noticer helps you to attain freedom.

As the noticer, your ego is not who you are. You do not identify the ego's pain as your pain. It's simply a pain in the ego.

- Getting Real keeps you present. By practicing the truth
skills, you become better at noticing when your mind tries
to take you out of your present experience and into a control pattern. You learn to interrupt your mind and to speak
what you notice, which brings you back into the present.

- Getting Real helps you stay with an experience to completion. Whenever you allow yourself to stay with an experience, resisting the mind's attempts to distract you and take
you out of the experience through various control patterns
and addictions, that experience will change. The way out
of a painful experience is by going into and through it.
This allows you to complete the unexpressed feelings from
your past so that you can move beyond them.

- Getting Real opens your mind up to new possibilities.
When you are not attached to a particular state, such as
comfort, you'll have no reason to resist *what is.* You'll be
able to perceive, take in, and relate to more of what is going
on in the moment. You will become more resourceful.
You'll see the options and possibilities (and even the dan-
gers) of a situation more fully and clearly, because your
attention will be freer. It won't be constricted by the tensing
and tightening that come from strategizing and watching
for danger.

- Getting Real fosters intimacy. To experience true intimacy
with another person, you must enter a realm of uncertainty
together. Getting Real gives you the ability to trust that
you can handle unplanned or unexpected outcomes.

- Getting Real enhances creativity and creative problem-
solving. One of the biggest blocks to creativity is having
your mind clogged with unfinished business stemming

from incomplete communications and inhibited self-expression. Practicing the ten truth skills keeps your mental energy flowing so your attention is available for dreaming up novel ways to do things. Another block to creativity is attachment to being right, safe, or certain. When you discover the joys of being real, unique, and open to surprise, your mind muscles relax so you can see things in new ways. Holding differences is another important prerequisite for solving complex problems. It allows you to see the mutually beneficial relationships between things that the mind might ordinarily think of as separate.

- Getting Real develops your intuition. Relating (versus controlling) helps you develop a very sensitive, even telepathic, resonance with your surroundings. This opens up your intuition — a resource that is likely to be helpful as the information explosion continues to boggle and confound the logical mind. By speaking aloud what you imagine, you are really testing your hunches. By being open to feedback, you see whether your imaginings are valid. And by being free and fluent in your self-expression, you allow hunches to emerge into the foreground of your conscious mind from the depths of your subconscious mind.

- Getting Real speeds up evolution. If you shorten the time between when a feeling, thought, or intuition is felt and when it is expressed and "gotten over," you move through your changes more quickly and with less unnecessary resistance. You find out more quickly if your decisions and actions are producing the results you want, so you can change your course in time to head off unintended outcomes.

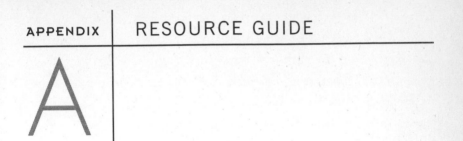

As a culture we are starting to wake up to our ingrained habits of denial and dishonesty. Getting Real (via the ten truth skills) is simply one expression of a trend in our society toward more authentic relating. In this appendix, I have listed books, tapes, and workshops that relate to the work of Getting Real. (If you have or know of a book or other resource that is not listed here but should be, feel free to send it to me for possible inclusion in future editions of this Resource Guide.)

Books

Blanton, Brad. *Radical Honesty: How to Transform Your Life by Telling the Truth.* New York: Dell, 1996.

————. *Practicing Radical Honesty: How to Complete the Past, Live in the Present, and Build a Future.* Stanley, VA: Sparrowhawk Publishing, 2000.

Bradshaw, John. *Family Secrets.* New York: Bantam, 1996.

Campbell, Susan. *The Couple's Journey: Intimacy as a Path to Wholeness.* San Luis Obispo, CA: Impact, 1980 (out of print but available from the author at www.susancampbell.com).

————. *Beyond the Power Struggle: Dealing with Conflict in Love and Work.* San Luis Obispo, CA: Impact, 1984 (out of print but available from the author at www.susancampbell.com).

————. *From Chaos to Confidence: Survival Strategies for the New Workplace.* New York: Simon & Schuster, 1995.

Dreaver, Jim. *The Way of Harmony.* New York: Avon, 1999.

Fritz, Robert. *Corporate Tides.* San Francisco: Berrett-Koehler, 1996.

Glickstein, Lee. *Be Heard Now.* New York: Broadway Books, 1998.

Hendricks, Gay, and Kathlyn Hendricks. *Conscious Loving.* New York: Bantam, 1990.

————. *The Conscious Heart.* New York: Bantam, 1997.

Katie, Byron. *All War Belongs on Paper* (available from the Work Foundation, P.O. Box 667, Manhattan Beach, CA 90267).

Kramer, Joel, and Diana Alstad. *The Guru Papers: Masks of Authoritarian Power,* Berkeley, CA: Frog, 1993.

Lowe, Paul. *The Experiment Is Over,* 1989 (available from the author at www.ineachmoment.com).

————. *In Each Moment.* Vancouver, BC: Looking Glass Press, 1998.

Mauer, Rick. *Beyond the Wall of Resistance: Unconventional Strategies That Build Support for Change.* Austin, TX: Bard Books, 1996.

Mindell, Arnold. *The Leader as Martial Artist.* San Francisco: HarperCollins, 1992.

Psaris, Jett, and Marlena Lyons. *Undefended Love.* Oakland, CA: New Harbinger, 2000.

Perls, Fritz. *The Gestalt Approach and Eyewitness to Therapy.* New York: Bantam, 1976.

Ross, Doug. *A Tao of Dialogue: A Manual of Dialogic Communication.* Blue Hill, ME: Medicine Bear Publishing, 1998.

Schutz, Will. *The Truth Option.* Berkeley, CA: Ten Speed Press, 1984.

Simmons, Annette. *A Safe Place for Dangerous Truths: Using Dialogue to Overcome Fear and Distrust at Work.* New York: Amacom, 1999.

Tolle, Eckhart. *The Power of Now.* Novato, CA: New World Library, 1999.

Free Newsletter

To receive Susan Campbell's on-line newsletter, *Uncertain Times,* send a blank e-mail to uncertaintimes-subscribe@yahoogroups.com.

Videotapes

Campbell, Susan. *How to Build a Loving Relationship.* Available by e-mailing me at drsusan@susancampbell.com. 1 hour, 1996.

CRM Films. *Riding the Wave: Strategies for Change.* Available by calling CRM at (800) 421-0833. 17 minutes, 1999.

Thinking Allowed. One-hour interviews with leading-edge thinkers (including Susan Campbell on "The Couple's Journey"). Contact www.spider12.lanminds.com/index.html.

Prices of tapes available at www.susancampbell.com

Workshops, Talks, and Retreats

Arica Institute, Dobbs Ferry, NY: (914) 674-4091

Brad Blanton, Radical Honesty Enterprises:
www.radicalhonesty.com

Susan Campbell, Getting Real Seminars: www.susancampbell.com

Dialogue Groups, Annette Simmons: e-mail
AnnetteGPC@aol.com

Gay and Kathlyn Hendricks, Hendricks Institute:
www.hendricks.com

Byron Katie, The Work Foundation: P.O. Box 667, Manhattan Beach, CA 90267

Landmark Education, Forum: www.landmarkeducation.com

The Learning Annex: www.thelearningannex.com

Paul Lowe: www.ineachmoment.com

Omega Institute: www.omega.org

Rowe Conference Center, Massachusetts: (413) 339-4954

Speaking Circles, Lee Glickstein: www.speakingcircles.com

Spirit Rock Meditation Center: www.spiritrock.org (Woodacre, CA)

Vipassana Meditation Retreats: www.dhiravamsa.org (U.S.A. and Europe)

Gift Items, Novelties, and Games

"For the Little Ones Inside" (deck of inspirational quotations). Available from the author: Robyn Posin, Box 725, Ojai, CA, (805) 646-4518, www.forthelittleonesinside.com

The Getting Real Card Game (a game of self-disclosure and fun for two to fourteen people, ages eight and up. Available from the author: Susan Campbell, 4373 Hessel Ct., Sebastopol, CA 95472, (707) 829-3646, e-mail: drsusan@susancampbell.com, www.susan-campbell.com

The Truth at Work Card Game (a team-building game for work groups). Available from the author: Susan Campbell, 4373 Hessel Ct., Sebastopol, CA 95472, (707) 829-3646, e-mail: drsusan@susancamp-bell.com, www.susancampbell.com, www.thegettingrealgame.com

Getting Real On-line Community

Join the Getting Real on-line discussion list to practice the ten truth skills with people from all over the world who have read this book or attended one of Susan Campbell's workshops. To subscribe, send a blank email to gettingreal-subscribe@yahoogroups.com.

COMMUNICATION GUIDELINES FOR GETTING REAL

B

We work with the following guidelines in the Getting Real workshops* and monthly Honesty Salons. At the start of each group, after a brief check-in circle, we read these guidelines aloud, each person taking a turn reading one of them. Then we all agree to use these guidelines to help us stay present and connected to one another.

If you wish to form your own group, you may find using these guidelines very helpful. Keep in mind, however, that these guidelines are only useful if everyone has read this book and played the Getting Real Card Game a few times, preferably with the same people. Participants need to understand what self-talk is and to be fairly fluent in sharing their self-talk. They also need to have some ability to give and receive experience-based feedback (as opposed to interpretive feedback); and they need to know the distinction between the two. If people have taken at least one Getting Real workshop and have read the book and played the card game, there is a greater likelihood that these guidelines can be put into practice. I am available by phone to coach people in starting their own Honesty Salons. I am

---

*If you copy and distribute these guidelines please note that it came from this book.

also available to come to your location to work with your group to get things started.

Here are the guidelines:*

1. Connect with the other(s) before speaking. Look into people's eyes. Feel your bodily sensations and your breathing.

2. Speak from your own experience: I feel, I want, I see, I notice, I observe, I think, I imagine, I like, I don't like, I appreciate you for..., I resent you for..., I fear, I'm angry, I feel hurt, I'm sad, I'm disappointed. Use I statements to keep yourself in your experience. When sharing resentment or appreciation, be specific about what the other said or did.

3. Be conscious of your intent: Is it to offer support, energy, or attention? To get support or agreement? To get the other to do something or feel something? To hurt or get back at the other or to prove the other wrong? Or is it to share feelings and thoughts in the interest of transparency or in order to get over them? Your intent is part of your message. Ask yourself: Is my intent to control or to relate?

4. Communicate about your here-and-now experience. Reveal your self-talk, such as, "I am saying to myself, 'I hope I'm coming across as genuine.'" If you are having a recollection, label it as that. For example, "Right now, I'm remembering my dad's face after he hit me." If you are carrying hurt or resentment about a past interaction, you can say, "I'm remembering the hurt I felt when you said..." or "I resent you for saying..."

5. In giving feedback, be concrete. Tell the person specifically what she did or said that triggered this response in you, using the form: "When you..., I felt (or thought or said to myself)..."

---

*Someone in the group needs to take responsibility for helping people stay true to these guidelines.

6. If you are judging someone, label it as a judgment: "I notice I'm judging you right now. What I'm thinking is..."

7. If you notice yourself getting triggered, say, "I notice I'm being triggered," or "I notice I'm having a reaction...."

8. If you are making an interpretation about a person, label it as an interpretation. For example, "My fantasy about you is that you're feeling sad" or "I imagine you're feeling sad."

9. Check in often with yourself, sensing what's happening in your body. Support your feelings with your breath.

10. Don't speak unless you are moved to do so. Do not answer a question if you don't feel like answering it. Just say, "I don't feel like answering that right now."

11. Be honest in your listening. Don't fake interest.

The premise of these guidelines is that you are responsible for your own experience. Whatever you are experiencing is a mirror of where you are in the moment. Your experience is uniquely yours. Validation by others doesn't make it right. Disagreement doesn't make it wrong. Your honest feedback or response is the greatest gift you can give to another person.

DESCRIPTION AND ORDERING INFORMATION FOR CARD GAMES

The Getting Real Card Game

This card game is for two to fourteen players, ages eight and up. The idea behind the Getting Real Card Game is that it's more fun to tell the truth than it is to lie, pretend, and conform to others' expectations. Playing the game offers you a chance to explore truth telling as a doorway to greater aliveness and self-trust. As you play, you'll be developing the ten basic truth skills described in this book. These truth skills will empower you to communicate more openly and to get over any unnecessary concern you may have about how other people may react to your honesty. During the game, you will be asked to share your self-talk, create your own "wild cards," and communicate with the intent to *relate,* not to *control.* The results are often profound, always provocative, frequently heartwarming, sometimes disturbing, but mostly hilarious.

Players take turns answering self-revealing questions. These questions are printed on the cards, which are placed in four different stacks, representing four levels of challenge. You get more points for answering the more challenging questions. After answering a question, you then ask for feedback from the other players. If you wish to pass on a particular question, you may share your in-the-moment self-talk instead of answering. You can play this game over and over with the same or different people. It gets richer, and people get funnier, the more you play it. The game can be played at various levels of self-disclosure, depending on the people involved. The instruction booklet includes suggestions for the host/hostess, or "game master," on how to customize the game for your particular group — so that it is challenging enough to be interesting, but not so challenging that people feel unsafe.

Here is some sample text from the cards:

Go around the room and say one thing you notice about each person.

What question would you not want to be asked on a first date?

What specific feedback do you have for the person whose turn it was just before yours?

What is the biggest lie you have ever told (or one of the biggest)?

Tell us about a situation in which you imagine being reluctant to tell the complete truth.

As a child, what career did you aspire to?

How safe do you imagine people feel telling you exactly what they are thinking?

Pick the person here whom you know best and say three words that describe your relationship to this person.

What were you like in high school?

The game consists of 250 cards and an instruction booklet. Cost: $25

WARNING: Playing this game may push the edges of your comfort zone.

Here's what a few people had to say about the game:

"I played the Getting Real Game with my family when I visited my parents for Thanksgiving. My three brothers and their wives and children were all there too. The ages ranged from ten to eighty-five. I got to know things about my brothers (we're all in our forties and fifties) that I never knew — like how they feel about their lives, their work, and their relationships, and their hopes, dreams, and regrets. It was so good for the kids to see their parents being so real. And the kids were great. In the "wild cards," they asked some deep questions about life and love that really challenged us and gave us a new understanding of the kinds of concerns they have. Now we play Getting Real whenever we all get together."

— psychologist, age fifty-nine

"I brought the game to my men's group. These are men in all walks of life — the building trades, farming, teaching, the arts. It was an amazing experience. Many of their responses brought tears to my eyes — sometimes because they were so moving, and sometimes because they were so funny! Playing the game together brought us to a new level of sharing with each other."

— teacher, age forty

"I asked some people over to play the game. I had some fears about how it would go. What I found out was that everyone there had been wishing for more connection with people. Playing the game together gave us that. We've played it together three times so far, and it's never the same. It seems to get better, more fun and interesting, every time."

— small business owner, age forty-six

The Truth at Work Card Game

The Truth at Work Card game is a game of self-expression, skill building, and fun for work groups. It offers work groups a lively, structured way to develop trust, thus enhancing the group's ability to make good decisions, take cooperative action, continually improve performance, and accept people for who they are. People learn that love and acceptance are powerful forces in bringing out each person's best. They also learn that constructive, challenging feedback can be delivered with respect, care, and humor.

The game, which is the result of more than twenty-five years of research on how to build high-performing teams, teaches such truth skills as the ability to distinguish between your actual experience and your beliefs or assumptions. It helps people be more present to the realities of their current situation. The game also focuses on improving group members' ability to speak, hear, and learn from other people about such important topics as trust, vision, mission, values, culture, individual strengths and challenges, decision making, conflict, personality styles, meetings, leadership, rewards, and coping with change. It is designed to be led by a trained group facilitator.

Like the Getting Real Card Game, it also presents players with questions written on cards and can be customized to fit the culture and comfort level of the group. You get more points for answering the more challenging questions. After answering a question, you then ask for feedback from the other players. If you wish to pass on a particular question, you may share your in-the-moment self-talk instead of answering.

Here is some sample text from the cards:

What are you passionate about?

What would you like to be valued, acknowledged, or given credit for?

Tell us something that you think might change our opinion of you.

Tell us about one of your most embarassing moments.

What is your truth in this moment?

What help do you need from others here to do your job better?

What help would you like to offer to anyone here to help them be more effective in his or her job?

Name one thing you think would improve our group's ability to deal with conflict.

In which instances while working here have you been rewarded or appreciated for your honesty?

If you could lay down some ground rules to make our meetings more effective, what would they be?

Who in this group do you wish you had a stronger relationship with?

Who here do you seek feedback from in the normal course of your job? Toward what end?

The game consists of 250 cards.

Cost: $90 (plus shipping and handling and facilitator's fee, if applicable)

Here's what a few people had to say about the game:

"We played the Truth at Work Card Game the night we all arrived before a three-day team-building retreat. It broke down barriers to trust and got us relating as human beings instead of as our roles. I think it gave our retreat a good jump-start, so we got more accomplished."

— manager, age thirty-five

"I brought Susan in to try the game out with our top team. I felt so much trust in the group after that. I found myself going to people and asking for their feedback — and really listening to them in a deeper way. I guess I'm just more relaxed around here now. We will definitely do this again."

— CEO, age fifty-five

Order Form

Name _____

Address _____

Phone _____

Fax _____

E-mail _____

Website _____

I am ordering ___sets of the Getting Real Card Game ($25) each.
I am ordering ___sets of the Truth at Work Card Game ($90) each.

Subtotal _____

Add 7 $\frac{1}{2}$% sales tax (CA res. only)_____

Add for shipping and handling_____
$6.00 first item, $2.00 thereafter

Total _____

Payment method: Check/Money Order_____

Credit Card #_____Expires_____

Send to: Susan Campbell
4373 Hessel Court
Sebastopol, CA 95472
Phone: (707) 829-3646
Fax: (707) 823-6789
E-mail: drsusan@susancampbell.com
Websites: www.susancampbell.com
www.thegettingrealgame.com

INDEX

ABOUT THE AUTHOR

Susan Campbell has written five previous books on interpersonal relationships: *Expanding Your Teaching Potential: Education for Participation in a Changing World* (Irvington, 1977), *The Couple's Journey: Intimacy as a Path to Wholeness* (Impact, 1980), *Earth Community: Living Experiments in Cultural Transformation* (Island, 1982), *Beyond the Power Struggle: Dealing with Conflict in Love and Work* (Impact, 1984), and *From Chaos to Confidence: Survival Strategies for the New Workplace* (Simon & Schuster, 1995). Her books have been translated into French, Spanish, Portuguese, Japanese, and German.

Susan and her Learning/Discovery approach to communication, conflict, and change are the subject of a twenty-minute professional training video produced in 1999 by CRM Films. The film and accompanying workbook are widely distributed to Fortune 500 companies and to government agencies. As an internationally known professional speaker and seminar leader, Susan is constantly in front of audiences. She publishes a newsletter entitled *Uncertain Times,* which she offers free to clients or anyone wishing to be on her e-mailing list. She is also creator of the two-day seminar, Getting Real, which she offers throughout the United States and abroad. And she hosts regular Honesty Salons one evening a month at her home. Susan lives in Sebastapol, California.

H J Kramer/New World Library is dedicated to
publishing books and audiocassettes
that inspire and challenge us to improve the quality
of our lives and our world.

Our books and tapes are available
in bookstores everywhere.
For a catalog of our complete library
of fine books and cassettes, contact:

H J Kramer/New World Library
14 Pamaron Way
Novato, CA 94949

Phone: (415) 884-2100
Fax: (415) 884-2199
Or call toll-free (800) 972-6657
Catalog requests: Ext. 50
Ordering: Ext. 52

E-mail: escort@nwlib.com
Website: www.newworldlibrary.com